Technology, Education
The TEC Se

Series Editor: Marcia C. Linn
Advisory Board: Robert Bjork, Chris Dede,
Carol Lee, Jim Minstrell, Jonathan Osborne, Mitch Resnick

Endorsements for
Rethinking Education in the Age of Technology

"Collins and Halverson offer a bold vision for bringing schools into the digital age—and for how technology can promote education beyond the schools."
—**Adam Gamoran,** dean of the University of
Wisconsin-Madison School of Education

"School is a troubled concept; Collins and Halverson are very clear about why and what we can do about it."
—**Roger Schank,** former professor at Yale and Northwestern, and author
of *Tell Me a Story* and *Lessons in Learning, e-Learning, and Training*

"Drawing on their decades of research in and out of schools, Collins and Halverson develop a penetrating and sweeping analysis of how technology is creating new challenges and opportunities for education today. A must read for parents, educators, or scholars interested in preparing future generations for this technology-soaked world."
—**Kurt Squire**, University of Wisconsin-Madison, author of
From Content to Context: Videogames as Designed Experience

"*Rethinking Education* is a tour de force. The authors cover wide terrain yet manage to synthesize their materials both broadly and deeply, providing sweeping (sometimes breathtaking) insights into the current predicament of education—the veritable tug-of-war being waged between the technology-rich everyday life of the digitally privileged and the backward-leaning industrial model of learning we call schools. I recommend this text for anyone serious about education not just as a topic in history, but also as an aspiration for future generations: education and sociology scholars, teachers, parents, designers, and lifetime learners themselves. Collins and Halverson may very well be the new 'Horace Mann' for today's increasingly globalized, networked, diverse 'flat' (Friedman) world."
—**Constance Steinkuehler,** University of Wisconsin-Madison, author of
Massively Multiplayer Online Games as an Educational Technology

"Rethinking the nature of education as it may blossom and grow outside of schools for all learners and throughout a lifetime is one of the central design challenges of our new century. In their charting of a dawning second educational revolution, Collins and Halverson illuminate how the values and opportunities of deeply social designs for technologies should and will expand learning environments beyond mainstream concepts of 'schooling'. Anyone who cares about education should read their book."
—**Roy Pea,** Stanford University, and author of
Technology, Equity, and K-12 Learning.

Rethinking Education in the Age of Technology

THE DIGITAL REVOLUTION AND SCHOOLING IN AMERICA

ALLAN COLLINS
RICHARD HALVERSON

FOREWORD BY
JOHN SEELY BROWN

Teachers College
Columbia University
New York and London

Published by Teachers College Press, 1234 Amsterdam Avenue, New York, NY 10027

Library of Congress Cataloging-in-Publication Data

Collins, Allan.
  Rethinking education in the age of technology : the digital revolution and schooling in America / Allan Collins, Richard Halverson ; foreword by John Seely Brown.
      p. cm. — (Technology, education-connections—The TEC Series)
  Includes bibliographical references and index.
  ISBN 978-0-8077-5002-5 (pbk. : alk. paper) — ISBN 978-0-8077-5003-2 (hardcover : alk. paper)   1. Education—Effect of technological innovations on—United States.
2. Educational technology—United States.   3. Educational change—United States.
4. Technological innovations—Social aspects—United States.   I. Halverson, Richard, 1939– II. Title.   III. Title: Digital revolution and schooling in America.
  LB1028.3.C636 2009
  370.285'4—dc22

                                                                          2009016308

ISBN 978-0-8077-5002-5 (paperback)
ISBN 978-0-8077-5003-2 (hardcover)

Printed on acid-free paper

Manufactured in the United States of America

16 15 14 13 12 11   8 7 6 5 4

Contents

Contents

8. How Schools Can Cope with the New Technologies — 112

Performance-Based Assessment — 113

Foreword

Before the industrial revolution, much of our education occurred at home or in schools that were often nothing more than one-room school houses. Teaching had not become a profession, and learning was a bit haphazard. I am nostalgic perhaps, but I find the notion of the one-room schoolhouse still intriguing and, ironically, suggestive of what learning in the networked age of the 21st century could more closely resemble than the schools of the industrial age.

In a typical one-room schoolhouse the students were both teachers and learners. Part of the time students "taught" those in the grade below and part of the time they learned from those above. The teacher, since she or he had all class levels together, couldn't really instruct as teaching is thought of today. She had to be an orchestrator of small learning communities— kids learning together from and with each other—and as such, learning was social, not didactic. As is well known, there is no better way to learn something than by teaching or explaining it to someone else.

The rise of the industrial revolution along with vast immigration to America put new demands on education. Since factories were the new order of the day, a factory-like form of education developed, staffed by professional teachers, which could scale and provide universal education. Education became systemized. This factory model of education actually worked relatively well in a world where change wasn't constant and skills learned could be applied for a lifetime.

But, in today's world, one of accelerating change, in which many skills become obsolete nearly as fast as they are learned, both schooling and learning are under siege. The factory model is struggling and the computer-based instructional technologies that showed such promise never really lived up to our expectations. If we shift our focus, however, from teaching to learning as well as from instruction to productive inquiry, the new social media and social networks start to allow a large-scale form of peer-based, social learning for the world of today's students. I am not saying that this kind of learning will replace schooling, but it does allow new forms of both formal and informal learning to emerge around the edges of formal schooling. Productive inquiry is now more possible than ever. Whatever your particular interest is, there is some niche community already formed on the network that you can join. The Internet provides a nearly infinite set of resources, in many languages, both visual and textual, to explore. These resources not only provide facts. They are also tools you can use to build things to tinker with, to play with, to reflect on, and to share with others. And most importantly, you will learn from other peoples' comments and from what they do with your creations.

I predict that these learning "edges" will cluster around the core of formal schooling, both informing and influencing each other, producing a form of co-evolution. With luck, from this interplay we will see a new culture of learning emerge, one that will set the foundation for learning in the 21st century, or as this book beautifully details, the second educational revolution.

John Seely Brown

Acknowledgments

We developed the ideas for this book when we taught a course together on the history of education reform at Northwestern University. Allan has continued to teach the course, and we thank all the students in the course over the years for their comments on previous drafts of the book. In particular, we would like to thank Le Zhong for a suggestion as to how to improve Chapter 5, which we incorporated in later drafts of the book, and Erica R. Halverson for her insightful comments on the initial drafts. Carol Kountz helped us decide what material to keep in the book and what material to delete. Shirley Brice Heath's comments on an earlier draft and suggestions for revision were invaluable. We also want to thank Donald A. Norman for his encouragement and suggestions for how to write the book to appeal to a general audience, the anonymous reviewers, and Janet Kolodner for their suggestions that led to extensive revisions to the manuscript.

Our series editor Marcia Linn was critical to bringing us to Teachers College Press and our editor there, Meg Lemke, worked very hard to make the manuscript presentable for teachers and a general audience. John Seely Brown was kind enough to write a foreword for the book, for which we are very grateful. Finally, we want to thank David Williamson Shaffer for his suggestions on how to publicize the book, and Larry Erlbaum, David Perkins, Roy Pea, and Barbara Means for all their help in finding a publisher.

Preface

I have not even intended to judge whether this social revolution, which I believe to be irresistible, is advantageous or disastrous for mankind. I have acknowledged that this revolution is already accomplished or about to be so and I have chosen among those people who have experienced its effects the one in which its development has been the most comprehensive and peaceful, in order that I may make out clearly its natural consequences and the means of turning it to men's advantage. I confess that in America I have seen more than America itself; I have looked there for an image of the essence of democracy, its limitations, its personality, its prejudices, its passions; my wish has been to know it if only to realize at least what we have to fear or hope from it. (de Tocqueville, pp. 23–24)[1]

Like de Tocqueville, we set out to describe an American revolution. It is the second educational revolution to occur in America, following almost 200 years after the revolution that took us from apprenticeship to universal schooling. It is brought on by all the new technologies that have been invented in recent years and it brings a challenge to schooling as the major venue where learning occurs. The revolution is by no means a finished work, just as democracy in America was not a finished work in 1831 when de Tocqueville visited America. Again like de Tocqueville, we try to look at this revolution with all its challenges and its promise. The revolution is advancing globally, but America appears to be at the leading edge, just as it was during the democracy revolution.

Who will benefit, ultimately, in the aftermath of this revolution? In America there is a commercial push to sell educational products to consumers who are looking for an edge up in the race for success. This means that technological products and services are popping up all over the American landscape. Education, once viewed as a public good with equal access for all, is now up for sale to those who can afford specialized services and computer programs.

The trouble with being in the vanguard of such a revolution is the problem it causes for people who are unable or unwilling to cope with the changes. As America stumbles ahead, new inequities and commercialization are creeping into the education system. Because of increasing disparities in income, we are seeing technological advantages to the wealthy that exacerbate their social and cultural advantages, which were already so apparent.

We have been advocates for advancing the use of technology in schools but this book is about how we see the very definition and experience of education radically changing under the pressure of a developing technological infrastructure. We recognize our biases from working as foot soldiers in the transformation of education in America, but we have stepped back from them in this book to take a big picture view.

We think schools have served America and the world very well. We greatly admire the teachers who have dedicated themselves to helping children from different backgrounds learn and thrive in a changing world. Schools have made invaluable contributions to the world's development, and we think they will continue to do so well into the future.

However, we think it is time that educators and policymakers start to rethink education apart from schooling. Education is a lifelong enterprise, while schooling for most people encompasses only the years between ages 5 and 18 or 21. Even when students are in school, much of their education happens outside of school. We all know that technology has transformed our larger society. It has become central to people's reading, writing, calculating, and thinking, which are the major concerns of schooling. And yet technology has been kept in the periphery of schools, used for the most part only in specialized courses.

We argue that there are deep incompatibilities between technology and schooling. Thus, it is no surprise that technology's main impact on learning is occurring outside of school. In consequence, we believe that policy leaders must rethink education both inside and outside of the school context.

The central challenge is whether our current schools will be able to adapt and incorporate the new power of technology-driven learning for the next generation of public schooling. If educators cannot successfully integrate new technologies into what it means to be a school, then the long identification of schooling with education, developed over the past 150 years, will dissolve into a world where the students with the means and ability will pursue their learning outside of the public school.

1

How Education Is Changing

We have all heard the stories about how education is changing:

The parents of a young mathematical whiz decide that he is not getting anything out of school. So they decide to teach him at home while letting him take gym classes in school. A retired engineer from AT&T is enlisted to introduce him to the wonders of educational software. He introduces the kid to many different software programs, such as Geometer's Sketchpad *and* Mathematica, *where the kid can push his mathematical knowledge to the limits. When he grows up, he represents the United States in the Mathematics Olympiad.*

Seymour Papert, a technology visionary, tells the story of how when his grandson was 3 years old, he developed a passion for dinosaurs. So his parents bought him lots and lots of videos about dinosaurs. He watched them over and over. As Seymour put it, "Before he could read, he learned much, much more about dinosaurs than I will ever know!"

A mid-career employee in an insurance firm is told by her boss that she would be a candidate for advancement to a managerial position if she got an MBA. So she decides to work for a master's degree at the University of Phoenix, an online university that now has more than 100,000 students. She works on courses at night and, after 2 years, completes her MBA degree, which enables her to move into management.

Michele Knobel tells the story of a teen whose passion is to make "animé music videos." He participates actively in the AniméMusicVideo.org web community, where he learns programming skills from fellow members. He is gaining something of a following online, as shown by the high number of YouTube

1

views of his "Konoha Memory Book," remixed by animating music with scenes from the Japanese animé Naruto. *The skills he is learning prepare him for careers in the digital and recording arts.*

Korean teens flock to Internet cafés in order to play online games such as Lineage. *They fuel a lucrative virtual economy, practice virtual trades, and engage in clan-based warfare. The South Korean government grows concerned when* Lineage *clan conflicts spill over into real-life street fighting.*

Brigid Barron tells the story of a boy named Jamal in Bermuda, who got excited when he took a computer science course in high school. He read several books on web design, and corresponded with one of the authors over the Internet. After he completed the course, he decided to start a business called Dynamic Web Design. An adult friend offered to share his office, and so Jamal designed a web page for him. The friend thought Jamal had real talent and encouraged him to pursue his business dream.

A teenager drops out of high school because he is bored with school. He decides to get various accreditations from Microsoft and Cisco, so that he can work as a computer programmer. He goes online to take courses that will prepare him for the accreditation exams, which he passes. These enable him to get a job in the programming department of a large bank in his city, where he studies the banking business from software modules that the bank developed for its employees.

A retired accountant decides to study painting after she retires, which she has wanted to do since she was young. She studies art through a correspondence course and takes up painting on her computer using a paint program she discovered through her course. After a couple of years, she is turning out beautiful computer paintings, which she thinks might be worth selling, so she sets up a web site where she advertises her work for sale to the world.

In his book Next, *Michael Lewis tells the story of how a 15-year-old named Marcus Arnold began giving legal advice on a web site called AskMe.com, where a variety of self-appointed experts provide answers to questions from people around the world. The 15-year-old had never read any law books, but he loved the law and had watched many TV shows involving legal matters. His answers were straightforward, so people found them more helpful than those by the many lawyers on the site. Eventually, he rose to be the top-rated expert on the legal advice section of the site.*

People around the world are taking their education out of school into homes, libraries, Internet cafés, and workplaces, where they can decide what they want to learn, when they want to learn, and how they want to learn. These stories challenge our traditional model of education as learning in classrooms. These new learning niches use technologies to enable people of all ages to pursue learning on their own terms.

At the same time, the public schools in America are facing a crisis. The public is demanding higher standards from K–12 schools with policies that limit the variety of learning opportunities. And communities are less willing to raise taxes for schools, because a smaller proportion of households have children of school age. Children raised on new media technologies are less patient with filling out worksheets and listening to lectures. Parents worry about a peer culture where drugs and violence are rampant, where the media market glorifies adolescent celebrities, and where school learning is belittled. On top of these problems, the best teachers are leaving high-poverty schools that need them most, because they can earn more money and respect in other districts or even in other occupations. Many teachers see little value in spending their time helping students prepare for standardized tests that they do not think measure real learning. Taken together, these stresses have pushed most schools to follow practices that reduce learning choices at the same time that technologies widen options.

Over the course of educational history, the success of universal schooling has led us to identify *learning* with *schooling*. Passing through school, from kindergarten to high school to college, has become a badge of success for countless Americans. The pervasiveness of schooling leads us to overlook the fact that the identification of schooling and learning has only developed in the last 150 years.

We see the question of where education is headed in terms of the separation of schooling and learning. We're not predicting the collapse of your local elementary school. Young people will not be forced to retreat behind computer screens to become educated. Rather, we see the seeds of a new education system forming in the rapid growth of new learning alternatives, such as home schooling, learning centers, workplace learning, and distance education. These new alternatives will make us rethink the dominant role of K–12 public schools in education as children and adults spend more time learning in new venues.

The clash between schooling and the new technologies is rooted in the historical emergence of universal schooling in America. The early institutional history of American schooling resulted in a network of durable organizational practices, such as age-grading, separating elementary and high schools, and admission and graduation expectations that protect a stable core of teaching and learning practices. This network has proven amazingly adaptive in protecting the basic practices of teaching and learning from changes in population, location, income, or size of school populations.

One chapter of this book provides a brief tour through the development of public schooling in America to show how the educational system changed radically during the Industrial Revolution of the 19th century. When people started working in factories, the existing practices for passing on knowledge, based on apprenticeship, broke down. The public schools in America were designed to offer a standard educational program to massive numbers of students from increasingly nonagricultural families.

In the mass-schooling model, the teacher is an expert whose job is to transmit that expertise to large groups of students through lecture, recitation, drill, and practice. The curriculum spells out what students are to learn and in what order, and testing is carried out to determine whether students have learned what was covered. If students have learned the appropriate content, they are allowed to advance to the next grade, acquiring as they advance a record of courses taken and grades assigned. The technologies undergirding this system are the textbook with its scope and sequence, the blackboard and overhead projector to support teacher explanations and display student work, the copier machine to reproduce handouts and worksheets, and most centrally, paper and pencil for recording and assessing student work. Together these practices and technologies reinforce each other and lead to an overall conservatism of practice.

Now we are going through another revolution on the same scale as the Industrial Revolution. It is variously called the Information Revolution or the Knowledge Revolution, and is fueled by personal computers, video games, the Internet, and cell phones. While the imperatives of the industrial-age learning technologies can be thought of as uniformity, didacticism, and teacher control, the knowledge-age learning technologies have their own imperatives of customization, interaction, and user-control. Knowledge-age technologies emphasize access to allow people to pursue their own interests and goals. Instead of accessing knowledge through visiting physical locations such as schools and libraries, people can find information on practically any topic and communicate with others wherever they are. They can also participate in games and activities that provide immediate feedback on their performance. Online, people can control what they do, who they communicate with, and even who they are.

The Knowledge Revolution has gradually transformed work over the course of the 20th century. There has been explosive growth in the numbers of technical, medical, legal, and financial workers. Shoshana Zuboff describes how a variety of jobs have changed to become much more knowledge-intensive.[1] She describes how the job of pulp mill operators, for example, has moved from steaming rooms where wood chips are made into paper to air-conditioned control rooms where the operators have to interpret what is happening by reading a variety of information displays. The work has changed from hands-on to inferential, or from concrete to abstract. Similarly, the job of secretary in many companies has changed from typing documents for superiors to handling interactions with people inside and outside the corporation. The job of farmer has changed from plowing and harvesting to purchasing and operating machinery, carrying out financial analyses, and marketing different products. The computerization of work puts a premium on skills of accessing, evaluating, and synthesizing information. Hence, in recent decades, the difference in pay between college-educated and non-college-educated has been growing.[2] To earn a decent wage in the future will require lifelong learning and expertise with information technologies.

At the same time the school system has become more stable, technology-based learning venues outside of school have been expanding rapidly. Modern technologies—in particular, video, computers, and networks—have been changing the ways we produce, consume, communicate, and think. These are having profound effects throughout the social, economic, and political spheres of society.

They are having equally profound effects on the ways we learn. If we look carefully, most of those changes in the way people acquire information are occurring outside of schools. Children watch hours and hours of television, where they can watch everything from *Sesame Street* to *South Park*. The number of parents who are schooling their children at home has exploded over the last 25 years. More and more parents are sending their children off to learning centers run by private companies to help their grades in school or to prepare for college entrance tests.[3] Home computers are almost as popular as microwaves and televisions, and in many homes children lead the way, showing their parents how to use computers for gaming, research, and networking.

As students enter the work world, computers guide their training for the different facets of their jobs. And they are more and more likely to take courses at a local college or adult education program or on the web to help them improve their skills or enrich their lives. Most of these things were simply not happening in the middle of the 20th century. Technology is moving education out of schools and into homes and workplaces, pre-schools and post-schools, after hours and after-after-hours.

There are deep incompatibilities between the demands of the new technologies and the traditional school. Technology makes life more difficult for teachers. It requires new skills that teachers often have not learned in their professional development. Further, the lockstep model of most classrooms undercuts the power of the new technologies to individualize learning. Teachers can feel that the endless amount of information available on the web undermines their classroom expertise. Much of what students pick up from the web is of doubtful reliability, and there are few widely accepted norms for how to evaluate it. Cell phones and video games are seen mainly as devices that distract students from classroom instruction. At least with textbooks and structured curriculum, teachers can know what the students are supposed to be learning. Teachers who embrace new technologies in their practice are regarded as mavericks, and are often left to seek out professional and curricular support on their own. Even as schools rush to incorporate technologies into their buildings, the traditional school classroom is very uncomfortable with these new subversive technologies.

As a result, schools have kept new digital technologies on the periphery of their core academic practices. Schools often provide computer labs, tech prep courses, and computer literacy and programming courses to help students learn about technology, but do not try to rethink basic practices of teaching and learning. Computers have not penetrated the core of schools, even though they have come to dominate the way people in the outside world read, write, calculate, and think. Since these practices are the bread and butter of traditional education, schools ignore computers at their peril.

The changes sparked by the Knowledge Revolution are neither all good nor all bad. We see many benefits to the kinds of education that technology affords, such as the ability of learners to pursue those topics of interest to them and to take responsibility for their own education. We also see many benefits in the successful history of traditional public schooling in America, which has provided extraordinary access to learning, status, and economic success for millions of students over the course of the past 2 centuries. But at the same time the roads to dystopia are also open. In particular, the new technologies can undermine both Jefferson's vision of educating citizens who can make sensible public policy decisions and Mann's vision of a society where everyone can succeed by obtaining a public education. Increasing the ability to personalize educational opportunities makes it possible for learners to focus on their own self-interest and gives a natural advantage to those who can afford the services.

Our fear is that social cohesion and equity inherent in the promise of public schooling will be undermined by this second revolution. Paradoxically, technologies that seem to create more opportunities for equity in learning may well serve to reinforce the widening economic gap. The challenge of technology-driven learning opportunities rests on the question of access. More and more people with means are able to purchase the computer technologies that lead to new media literacies. One of the great promises of the traditional school system was to engage all students with common learning technologies. The different access in homes limits the abilities of schools to equitably distribute access to new learning technologies. We hope that by revealing the larger pattern of what is happening, we will make it possible for society to ward off the dangers and exploit the possibilities of new technologies.

THE STRUCTURE OF THE BOOK

Chapters 2 and 3 consider the debate between technology enthusiasts and technology skeptics. We think that the skeptics are correct in that there are deep incompatibilities between technology and schooling, but that the enthusiasts are correct in that education must change to stay relevant in the wake of the Knowledge Revolution. As we mentioned in the preface, we have been proponents of technology, and while we consider the skeptics' points fully, we also hope to convince readers of the opportunities and value of technology in learning. We see the response to the new technologies taking place mostly outside of schools as they are currently constituted, and we argue that we need to rethink schooling in the light of the new technologies.

Chapter 4 puts the current debate in context by considering the revolution in education that occurred when America moved from an apprenticeship-based system to a school-based system. Our argument is that this earlier transformation of education was fostered by a number of events, but it was precipitated by the Industrial Revolution. We are now going through a social revolution of similar magnitude, the Knowledge Revolution, which is bringing on another transformation in education toward lifelong learning. In Chapter 5, we discuss the seeds of the new education system that we see forming around us.

Chapter 6 describes critical differences among the three eras of education: the apprenticeship era that preceded the Industrial Revolution, the public schooling era that is slowly fading from the scene, and the lifelong-learning era that we are now entering. Chapter 7 considers what may be lost and what may be gained as we face a new future for education. Chapter 8 describes how schools can best capitalize on the opportunities that technology affords, and Chapter 9 describes what the educational revolution means more generally for society. Finally, in Chapter 10, we discuss the different aspects of education that require rethinking as we move from an education system centered on schooling to a system where people engage in learning throughout their lives.

In this book, we appear neither as advocates nor opponents of the new technologies. Rather, we want to observe what is happening, taking a historical perspective on the relation of schooling, learning, and technology. What will happen to the relation of computers and education is not in any sense inevitable. In fact, it is at critical times of change that the actions of particular individuals and groups have the most impact. The advent of the industrial age opened a window for Horace Mann and his contemporaries to shape the American education system of today. We again find ourselves at such a window of opportunity, where there is a battle raging between conventional and revolutionary venues for learning. There are many educational visionaries alive today. Not all of their dreams will succeed, but a few may capture the moment with the right idea and the right approach to change the future of education.

2

The Technology
Enthusiasts' Argument

Developments in technologies have often played a critical role in bringing about social and institutional change. Enthusiasts predict that the sweeping technological changes experienced in the worlds of business and entertainment must also take place in schools. Hence, many educators and technologists have made predictions as to how the processes of teaching and learning will be transformed by the new information technologies. There are two arguments that technology enthusiasts make as to why new technologies will revolutionize schooling. One is that the world is changing and we will need to adapt schooling to prepare students for the changing world they are entering. The other is that technology gives us enhanced capabilities for educating learners, and that schools should embrace these capabilities to reshape education. Enthusiasts have argued that embracing these two ideas will radically transform the way schools educate students.

THE CHANGING WORLD

New technologies are transforming every aspect of work: reading and interacting with the web; writing memos and sending email; computing with spreadsheets and statistical analysis programs; analyzing problems with data visualization tools; creating social networking sites; marketing with digital video tools; making presentations with PowerPoint. Reading, writing, calculating, and thinking are what education is all about. Yet schools are stuck using 19th-century technology, such as books, blackboards, paper, and pencils. Computers are not at the core of schools. They are used mainly for special courses in schools, such as programming, tech prep, and business applications, or for basic computer literacy. Students do not do most of their work in computer environments, unlike workers in modern offices and factories.

Enthusiasts argue that trying to prepare students for the 21st century with 19th-century technology is like teaching people to fly a rocket ship by having them ride bicycles. The technologies used at work and at school are getting further and further out of sync, and enthusiasts think that this gap between the old and the new technologies will force schools to adjust and incorporate new methods into the core practices of teaching and learning.

How We Think Is Changing

Technologies have evolved over the centuries to make sophisticated work more accessible to the common person. Some of the earliest tools, such as the wheel and the plow, were used to grow crops and make clothes. The Industrial Revolution was driven by a new set of power tools (e.g., engines and machines) that were used to enhance human muscle labor. The current Knowledge Revolution is driven by a new set of computer tools that empower people's minds rather than their bodies. As John Seely Brown argues, "Tools drive science. Not theory, not experiment; it's the tools. And it's this that has made the computer such an incredible force for scientific innovation. For example, the ability of the computer to crunch unbelievable amounts of information; to design and fabricate micromachinery; to link disparate technologies into networks; to create new materials with new properties; and to visualize what's going on in complex interaction has completely changed the speed and nature of innovation."[1] These new tools are reshaping the nature of work from a reliance on physical labor to cultivating the intellectual ability of ordinary people to interact with sophisticated symbol systems.

Enthusiasts like Brown argue that competent adults will need to master computer tools to accomplish their tasks in the future. Much of human knowledge has already found its way onto the web. People will need to develop skills to find the information they are looking for, to evaluate its usefulness and quality, and to synthesize the information they glean from the different sources they locate. Basic composition is being replaced by production of multimedia documents, which include text, graphics, photographs, video, animations, simulations, and visual displays of data. Workers will need to learn how to understand and produce in all these different communication media. Calculating has already moved from pen-and-paper computation to designing spreadsheets, managing complex databases, and using statistical analysis programs. One complex computer tool,

Mathematica, carries out all the algorithms that are taught up through graduate school, much more efficiently than students ever will. In fact, most thinking in the world, whether it is making airline reservations, controlling
airplanes, troubleshooting complex equipment, designing new artifacts,
exploring massive datasets to find patterns, and producing artistic products, is enhanced by computer tools. They are instrumental in all the activities that are central to thinking and learning.

Computer tools greatly extend the power of the ordinary mind in the
same way that the power tools of the Industrial Revolution extended the
power of the ordinary body. No one will be able to solve complex problems or think effectively in the coming world without using digital technologies. The presence of new technologies in the workplace has pushed
production in unanticipated directions by creating a culture of technology
dependence and innovation. Integrating new technologies in the workplace
created a cycle that established the conditions for subsequent new technology adoption. Just as reading was made necessary by the printing press
and arithmetic by the introduction of money, so computer technologies are
changing the very ways we think and make sense of the world.

How We Communicate Is Changing

One of the longest-running trends in history is the movement from
communities of place to *communities of interest*. Traditionally, community
refers to the town or neighborhood in which you live. This is the notion of
a community of place. It is the only community with which most people
interacted up through the 1600s. For example, in the Middle Ages, people
seldom traveled, and rarely had much contact with people who lived more
than 10 miles from where they were born. People got to know one another
very well, and spent their whole lives with others who shared the same
experiences, values, and beliefs about the world. Communities of place rely
on familiarity with folkways and circumstances to make communication
rich and localized.

Communities of interest, such as scientific societies, teacher unions,
orchid fanciers, and rock musician fan clubs, have arisen as a new basis
for communication. They are not bound by locality—indeed, many have
members around the globe. Technologies loosened the place-based community boundaries. The horse and stirrup started taking people farther
afield, and that distance was extended successively by the carriage, the ship,
the automobile, and the airplane. The book and the letter began to bring

knowledge about faraway places to more and more people, engendering both new ideas and a longing to travel. The telephone, radio, and television have greatly extended our knowledge and contact with the rest of the world. And in recent decades, the Internet is further extending people's contact with a world beyond their local community.

Consider the typical American professional at the turn of the 21st century. Let us say Kate is an engineer, but she could be a lawyer, researcher, or consultant, and she might work for a corporation, partnership, university, or nonprofit organization. We assume Kate represents where the world is headed. She works with people from many different cultures (e.g., Finland, China, Lebanon), often communicating with them at a distance through phone, email, and video conferences. She has her own web site and she accesses much of the information she works with from the web.

Much of her time is spent traveling to different places to work on specific jobs with other people from her organization. She belongs to professional organizations and she regularly attends national meetings and occasionally international meetings, with side trips to places she would like to visit. She has changed jobs a few times, moving from city to city. Hence, many of the friends she developed along the way now live elsewhere. In fact, she has more close friends in other places than she has in the city where she lives. But she keeps in touch by visiting them—for example, when a business conference takes her near a friend's home, by phoning when the mood strikes her, and updating her Facebook page.

But what technology gives, it can also take away. The time Kate spends communicating with people around the world may take away from her participation in her local community. She does not interact much with her neighbors, nor does she belong to any local associations or clubs. She may well use Craigslist.org to shop locally for goods and entertainment, or use the web to find out the best local clubs. Even these tools, though, allow her to explore her surroundings based on her interests, rather than based on the familiarity of shared surroundings characteristic of a community of place. She has become, in short, a person who interacts with the world, but not with her local community. In this regard, she is just the opposite of the person in medieval times.

Kate has to deal with people through a variety of media, as well as face-to-face communication. They have interests in common, but do not share the same backgrounds. Often, in fact, she may have to work with people from other cultures to accomplish projects in her work. Communication becomes more difficult because they do not share the same background, and often the medium of communication is impoverished as compared to face-to-face communication. Misunderstandings often arise in emails and dating sites, because many of the cues people rely on in face-to-face communication are absent.

As Mimi Ito, Kevin Leander, and Gail Boldt have argued, people are now using networked digital media for their ongoing business and social exchange.[2] Teens are leading the way in using new digital media to blur the boundaries between personal communication, work, and learning. These authors argue that mastering digital media is giving rise to a new media literacy. The new literacy extends the symbolic decoding and manipulation skills of traditional print media by integrating video, images, music, and animation comprehension that give rise to new kinds of production. Teens who are creating web pages with animated computer graphics and sound, remixing images to develop music videos, participating in web chats and forums, and writing their own blogs are engaged in developing a sophisticated media literacy not taught in schools.

To prepare students to communicate in this emerging world requires not simply the traditional reading and writing, but learning how to communicate using different media with people who do not share the same assumptions. Sometimes this means reading multimedia documents that come from different sources. Other times, this means communicating with people via the Internet in different contexts, such as design projects, negotiation, and problem solving. Internet communication may involve email, social network sites, chat rooms, video conferencing, and shared workspaces: Students need to learn to communicate in all these different contexts. Many teachers are working to integrate these new communities-of-interest technologies into their classrooms. Teachers are beginning to use learning management sites, such as Moodle, to create new opportunities for students to interact and do homework, and blogs to reflect on lessons as they are taught. Technology enthusiasts want schools to embrace the possibilities of new technologies in the many ways that are occurring outside of school.

ENHANCED CAPABILITIES FOR EDUCATING LEARNERS

Enthusiasts suggest that putting students in situations where computer tools will be necessary to solve complex problems will kickstart schools to change basic instructional practices. Since simply putting computers into schools, as in the 1980s and 1990s, did not produce the revolution, enthusiasts have now turned to more sophisticated implementation models, such as the design of interactive learning environments. Learning environments are computer programs where learners are put in new situations and given appropriate tools and supports to learn how to deal with those situations. Sometimes these are personalized tutoring programs and sometimes several people may be learning together. There are a variety of capabilities that these interactive learning environments bring to education that schools cannot easily provide. We will consider a number of these, to give the flavor of how technologists see education evolving.

Just-in-Time Learning

The notion of "just-in-time learning" is that whenever you need to learn something in order to accomplish a task, you can find out what you need to know. The most basic example of just-in-time learning is a well-designed computer program help system, which gives the advice you need just as you are engaged in a complex task. There are many examples of how the Internet can provide this kind of help. For example, you can learn to invest in the stock market by taking a web-based mini-course on the stock market. If you need to use a spreadsheet for a task you have to accomplish, an online spreadsheet tutor can get you started and help you as you do the task. If you want to buy a car, dozens of web sites offer prices, reviews, comparisons, dealer locations, lease rates, and trade-in values. These examples illustrate how just-in-time learning can come in big chunks or little chunks, depending on the learner's needs and desires.

Enthusiasts argue for just-in-time learning as the counter to the school strategy of trying to teach everything one might need to know someday. Many Americans spend 15–20 years in school learning things that they may or may not use later in life. In fact, we have been extending schooling gradually over the last 150 years, so that what is taught is becoming more and more remote from the time when it might be used in some real-world context.

The evidence has been piling up in recent years that adults forget most of what they learn in school. Philip Sadler found that when he asked Harvard seniors at graduation, "What causes the phases of the moon?" only three of 24 knew the correct answer. And when he asked, "What causes the seasons?" only one of 24 knew the correct answer, even though this was taught in elementary school.[3] Similarly, studies have found that only a third of adults know how to convert between systems of measurement and calculate with mixed units, such as hours and minutes.[4] Nor can most adults add and multiply fractions, or remember when the American Civil War occurred. These are all facts and procedures that we learned in elementary or middle school, but with no reason to use the knowledge in everyday life, most of us forget that we ever learned them. Just-in-time learning attempts to tie what is learned to its use in the world. Of course, it may be forgotten again, but it can always be relearned if needed, just in time.

The skills necessary for just-in-time learning are more skill-based than fact-based. Cultivating the ability to ask good questions (maybe in the form of a Google search!) is more valuable, from the enthusiasts' perspective, than learning a lot of basic facts. The idea behind just-in-time learning is to develop the skills that allow learners to find the right information anywhere, not just in classrooms with teachers.

Technologies provide the just-in-time learner with the kinds of information resources that can provide help when it is required. For example, one graduate student we know learned about investment strategies from a tutorial on the Motley Fool web site after inheriting money from a deceased parent. Enthusiasts argue that integrating just-in-time strategies into school curricula will loosen the rigidity of the traditional curriculum and create a legitimate space for learning technologies in the classroom.

There are good examples of how nontechnological just-in-time learning principles are influencing the design of classroom learning. Textbook designs, for example, have taken on the rich, mixed-media appearance of web pages, and provide in-depth explanations of concepts, historical reminders, and illustrations of how the concepts discussed at that point in the lesson might be used. Still, because most classroom teaching is done without digital media devices, the textbook implementation of just-in-time learning can become a bloated version of everything-at-once learning. Enthusiasts argue that once computer technologies become ubiquitous in schools, just-in-time learning strategies can come into their own.

Customization

One of the major effects of technology proliferation has been the ability to cater to individual preferences. People can download the music they want to hear and the movies and videos they want to see from the Internet. They can find almost any information they want on the web. More and more, web sites use sophisticated data analysis and "push technologies" to cater to the online identity of a consumer. From listservs to RSS news blogs, to E-bay and Amazon.com, sites offer people access to what they want when they want it. While major media sources still exercise significant control over what we see and hear, the Internet has loosened the hold of radio, TV, publishers, and theaters on our information options. If technology knows your interests and abilities, it can provide help when you need it, choose news and information of interest to you, and explain things in terms you will understand.

Information technologies have greatly enhanced the ability to define and exploit niche markets and connect people with communities and products of interest. The marketing information company Claritas has determined that most Americans belong to one of 62 zip code–defined clusters such as "Young Influentials" or "Smalltown Downtown." In 2008, Young Influentials, for example, were an ethnically diverse group of renters without kids, had a household income of $48,000, liked to play racquetball, read *Vibe* magazine and watched *King of the Hill* and *Family Guy* reruns. Such information helps companies, political parties, and special interests target their messages to likely customers.

Individuals also use information technology to customize their search for knowledge and products. Amazon.com indexes your past purchases against an immense network of other consumers to suggest products that may interest you. Engaging in online commerce through sites such as eBay.com allows customers to rate and review the reputation of vendors, and for vendors to assess the reliability of customers. Visitors to epinions.com can access other people's opinions on a wide variety of topics, and have the opportunity to vote on the quality of the opinions offered. Interactive video systems such as Tivo remember the programs you watch in order to suggest what you might like to see. Prior interaction helps the technologies "know" your interests and abilities, provide help when you need it, choose news and information of interest to you, and explain things in terms you will understand. This kind of personalization of network technology is in its infancy, but it will become more and more pervasive as the new technologies mature.

In recent years, the web has expanded to include advice, information, and opinion sites on almost any topic imaginable. The explosion of blogging allows anyone to publish personal and topical thoughts on the web, and also provides a platform for people with mutual interests to share information. As the speed of Internet connections increases, the traditional rules for accessing copyrighted media are brought into increasing conflict with Internet traditions of open access to information. Even as centralized peer-to-peer exchange sites, such as Napster, are shut down through legal action, decentralized sites, such as LimeWire and Kazaa, that share files directly between computers, spring up to help users exchange digital media. Cable and tele-communication companies are scrambling to create viable systems for down-loading whatever books, music, or videos you want.

Enthusiasts believe that customization offers great possibilities to en-hance people's learning. For example, Charles Stallard and Julie Cocker in their book *The Promise of Technology in Schools* envision that 10 years from now people will have their own computer-based personal learning assis-tants, which store records about their learning history in order to guide their learning.[5] They also believe that children growing up in a digital world will be so used to making choices in their lives that they will demand personalized learning choices. Hence, they seem to think that the days of standards-based education are numbered.

Interestingly, the press for customization of learning in schools is com-ing from another nontechnological innovation—special education. The special education Individualized Education Plan (IEP) aims to custom-ize learning to the needs of the individual student. From a technological perspective, though, the IEP has several problems. First, the learning customization is done *for* the student by interested adults, and second, the learning that is customized involves selecting from the regular school edu-cation program. In short, the IEP does not yet achieve the goals of learner-directed customization foreseen by technology enthusiasts, but it does represent a step in the direction away from the traditional standardized organization of classroom teaching and learning. Once technologies become commonplace in schools, teachers can build on interventions like the IEP to bring customized learning to more students.

One of the rules of adult education is that you can't teach adults some-thing that they are not interested in and don't see the point of learning. Like adults, young people are becoming less and less willing to learn what some-body else thinks is best. They want to decide what is of value to them. They are beginning to demand that they decide what they need to learn. Enthu-siasts believe that the ultimate effect of customization technologies will be to break the lockstep of school curricula.

Learner Control

Enhanced learner control is the counterpart of customization. Mod-ern technologies, particularly the web, are moving control away from cen-tralized sources. This is sometimes referred to as a shift from broadcasting to narrowcasting. In the era when a few companies, such as *Time*, CBS, and the *New York Times*, controlled the production and distribution of media, content could be controlled at the source and distributed widely, so that most people were reduced to media consumers. However, as sources of knowledge are becoming distributed, many people become both producers and consumers. In the 2008 election coverage, for example, sites such as fivethirtyeight.com, the dailykos.com, and realclearpolitics.com used the perspectives of thousands of citizens who followed the candidates across the country to make the news stories that were reported in the network news hours. These blogging/news sites open up new possibilities for participant-controlled news coverage.

Information technologies continue a long historical arc for freeing access to information. When Luther rebelled against the Catholic Church, he translated the Bible into German so that everyone could read it. He believed that individual people needed to be able to interpret the scriptures for themselves. Luther's translation relied upon the invention of the printing press, which made it possible to distribute his translation widely to the people. In fact, the printing press helped undermine the authority of the Church and began the long process of turning control of what was learned over to the people.

Schooling was developed as an institution to convey traditional knowledge to communities. Educators control what people learn by defining the curriculum in schools. The standards and assessment movement that culminated in the No Child Left Behind Act is the latest attempt to define what everyone should learn. Enthusiasts argue that as new technologies, like the printing press before them, enable people to take control of their own learning, people will decide what would be valuable to them and what they want to learn. They can decide how long they want to spend and what help they think they need. They are gaining more and more control over their own learning, both in big ways and in small ways. Hence, the imperative of technology is toward more learner control, and schools are fighting a losing battle to control what students learn. Technology enthusiasts think that as people decide to take control of their own education, schools will be pressured to embrace the technologies that make learner control possible.

Interaction

The interactivity of new media technologies provides a number of capabilities that can enhance education. As is evident from the popularity of computer games, interactivity can be very engaging. In fact, this is why drill and practice games, such as typing tutors and *Math Blaster*, can entice children to learn content that they might otherwise consider "boring." Enthusiasts believe that by providing even more sophisticated dynamic interaction, computer-based learning environments are likely to make education much more engaging.

Interaction also allows learners to see the consequences of their actions. In this way, they have their expectations and predictions confirmed or disconfirmed, and can try different courses of action to evaluate their relative effectiveness. In fact, there have been studies by Colette Daiute that demonstrate that children using word processors write better, because they can read their typed words, whereas they cannot easily read their own handwriting. Hence, they get immediate feedback on how they are doing, which they can easily modify using a word processor.[6] Engaging in online writing activities, such as fan fiction sites, provides access to legitimate audiences that challenge writers to improve their work.[7]

James Paul Gee's work on learning with video games suggests that computer feedback need not take the simple form of rewarding or punishing actions. Complex games give users rich feedback on the consequences of a series of actions or a strategy for interaction. To succeed in the games, users need to comprehend what this feedback means, and take the lessons of their experience into account in future play.[8]

Technology enthusiasts believe that when learners are given immediate feedback on their actions they are much more likely to learn what to do correctly. Computer tutors, such as the algebra and geometry tutors developed by John Anderson and his colleagues, observe learners carefully as they work to solve problems, and give immediate feedback when they are in trouble.[9] These tutors have been shown to be more effective than classroom teaching due to their ability to provide immediate feedback to learners. Enthusiasts believe that the interaction computers provide will change expectations for learning in subtle ways that schools will need to replicate.

Scaffolding

Developing a successful learning environment often means providing scaffolding for learners to engage in difficult tasks. Scaffolding is the support that a system provides learners in carrying out different activities. For example, a system designed to teach electronic troubleshooting structured the tasks to increase slowly in difficulty and offered hints when the student did not know what to do.[10] Another system designed to teach multidigit addition and subtraction modeled the carrying and borrowing of numbers with voice-enhanced animation.[11] A system designed to teach algebraic manipulation carried out the low-level chores, such as arithmetic calculations, so the learner could concentrate on the higher-level, executive tasks of deciding what to do.[12] Scaffolding takes many different forms, which enable learners to carry out tasks that are beyond their capabilities. In the best-designed systems, scaffolding fades naturally, as students need less support and they are able to do the tasks on their own.

Computer games also excel at providing scaffolded task designs that ease players into complex tasks. Games such as *Rise of Nations*, for example, strip down a busy interface to allow players to master the basic moves of game play, then introduce more options as players gain mastery. Enthusiasts argue that the design principles of such games could be adapted to structure the learning of more traditional, school-based content.

The organization of schooling already provides many forms of scaffolding. For example, age-grading and curricula that gradually increase in complexity take the capacities of learners into account. Textbooks also provide initial help that fades with the increasing complexity of the material. However, enthusiasts believe that with so many students to support, teachers do not have time to provide the individual scaffolding that students need. The recent movement for teachers to provide different kinds of lessons based on assessments of student needs, moves in the direction of individualized scaffolding. But even when such differentiation is done well, teachers find time to work with individual students at the expense of time needed for other students and tasks. Students who struggle at school are sometimes reluctant to ask for help for fear of being stigmatized as a slow learner.

Personalized scaffolding provided by computers comes without criticism and without others knowing that the student needs help. Offloading some of the instruction on well-designed computer tutors could support learning at whatever level students need.

Games and Simulation

Computers enable technologists to create scenarios where learners are given tasks in simulated environments that embody the kinds of knowledge and skills the learners will need in the real world. Simulations allow players to practice risky behaviors with limited real-world consequences. Through simulations, learners may have to diagnose a disease, troubleshoot a malfunctioning circuit, or put together a television news program.

One such simulation, built by Roger Schank and his colleagues, teaches genetics by having learners try to determine whether couples are likely to have children with a genetic disease.[13] In order to advise the couples, learners must find out how different genetic combinations lead to the disease and run tests to determine the parents' genetic makeup. There are scaffolds in the system to support the learners, such as various recorded experts who offer advice. Other simulations Schank's group built support learners in a wide variety of challenging tasks, such as solving an environmental problem or putting together a news broadcast about a historical event. These simulations make it possible to embed cognitive skills and knowledge in the kinds of contexts where they are to be used. So people learn not only the basic competencies they will need, but also when and how to apply these competencies.

Another kind of simulation occurs in *Biologica*, developed by Paul Horwitz and his colleagues to teach the basic processes of genetics.[14] *Biologica* presents a series of problems for learners to solve that involve reasoning about how different biological levels interact (i.e., genes and alleles, chromosomes, animal features such as wings, and populations). The problems involve fictional dragons that illustrate the basic rules that Mendel first discovered with peapods. *Biologica* starts with simple problems, which gradually increase in difficulty.

Chris Dede and his colleagues have built a simulation environment called *River City*, where learners guide an avatar through the city, trying to figure out why people are getting sick.[15] There are three diseases rampant in the city: One is water-borne, one insect-borne, and one is infectious. Learners can ask people they encounter what they know, inspect hospital records and question health workers, collect data about insects and water quality, and finally run tests to see what happens when they try to correct a problem. This requires the learners to systematically collect data and form hypotheses about what could be causing people to get sick.

Enthusiasts argue that simulation is the key to letting learners explore new situations. Simulations allow learners to try out different courses of action, and see the consequences of their choices. That is, they can ask "What if?" questions, and explore different possible solutions to problems. In this way, learners gain the ability to consider different possibilities and the flexibility to deal with contingencies. Such realistic tasks force learners to figure out what to do. They allow learners to take on roles in novel situations, something that is largely missing from school. These situations can be structured so that easier tasks arise before harder tasks.

Video games use the narrative devices of roles and plots to draw players in with the immersive aspects of simulations. Many games exploit real-world situations and physical rules, but allow players to take on new roles and engage in adventures outside everyday experience. James Paul Gee describes how video games draw players into roles that may conflict with everyday values and encourage players to notice the gap with their own beliefs. In games such as *Mass Effect* or *Command and Conquer,* for example, players take the roles of different sides in complex wars. To succeed in the game, players must understand the resources and capabilities of each side in the conflict, and then switch sides to take on the perspective of the enemy. Such role switching gives players the rare opportunity to see a conflict from multiple perspectives. Kurt Squire's augmented-reality gaming work takes interaction to a further level by blending social interaction with GPS-guided learning. Augmented reality environments challenge players to use scientific and historical reasoning as they solve local environmental and social issues.[16]

The constraints of these simulations take on a new dimension when players interact with one another in online play. Massively multiplayer online games (MMOGs), such as *World of Warcraft* and *Star Wars: Galaxies,* allow players to build characters and resources in sophisticated simulated worlds with market economies and self-policing communities. The vitality of these games depends upon players co-creating the world they inhabit. This interactive "world building" requires a wide range of social behaviors necessary for game success. The emergence of social roles and interaction seen in MMOGs provides a laboratory for researchers to study the evolution of economic and social systems.

Constance Steinkuehler's research points toward how these environments require advanced players to use scientific reasoning and complex leadership skills to succeed. [17] Sites such as *NeoPets* and *Club Penguin* provide simple video games that involve motor skill coordination and pattern matching to immerse children in a virtual economy based on character customization. MMOGs bring video game play closer to real-world interaction, and point to a future of how virtual-world interaction might be structured.

Enthusiasts such as Schank, Horwitz, Dede, and Gee argue that working with games and simulations makes learning more interesting. The tasks can be made very engaging, and the conditions for applying the knowledge are clear to the students. The enthusiasts contend that this is a problem with schools, where students are learning things that they have no idea how to apply.

Though innovative teachers often find ways to embed learning in meaningful tasks, much of school is like learning tennis by being told the rules and practicing the forehand, backhand, and serve without ever playing or seeing a tennis match. Students are taught algebra and parsing of sentences without being given any idea of how algebra and parsing might be useful in their lives. That is not how a coach would teach you to play tennis. A coach might first show you how to grip and swing the racket, but very soon you would be hitting the ball and playing games. A good coach would have you go back and forth between playing games and working on particular skills. The essential idea in teaching skills is to tightly couple a focus on accomplishing real-world tasks with a focus on the underlying competencies needed to carry out the tasks. Although real-world tasks for math and writing are difficult to re-create in schools, enthusiasts argue that simulations allow students to feel what it might be like to write for a political campaign or build a bridge.

While tying skills to practical outcomes is one way to apply the lessons of simulations to learning, simulations demonstrate that immersion in a complex, challenging environment can be valuable learning opportunity in itself. The inherent attraction of most video games, for example, is not based on possible practical outcomes, but rather on the fascination and continuous challenge of competing in a rule-governed world. In his effort to describe the psychology of optimal experience, Mihaly Csikszentmihalyi describes "flow" as a state of consciousness in which the distinctions between the subject and the object are blurred through immersion in engaging activity.[18] While parents decry the thousands of hours children spend playing video games, players report that these simulations create flow-like experiences that can be powerful learning opportunities.

Consider the contrast of watching a student do middle school math homework with the same student playing the football video game *Madden*. Working through the math problems is often a grinding task isolated from either applying or understanding the "big concepts" of math. The main goal of math homework is to get it done. In playing *Madden*, however, the student will use many of the same analytic skills to maintain a salary cap, guess future player performance standards, and calculate odds for success while assembling a football team roster. The flow state of game play integrates skill development and usage in a seamless experience that, unfortunately, masks the complexity of the skills required for successful game play. Enthusiasts argue that because schools explicitly draw out the sub-skills involved in complex learning, the resulting learning environments limit opportunities for flow. The freedom to learn the constraints of a complex world through self-guided exploration is a learning capacity that remains out of the reach of our current system of schooling.

Multimedia

Bringing together print, video, and audio into multimedia presentations provides a new opportunity for communicating information. A number of writers have tried to characterize the shift that occurred with the invention of the printing press as society moved from traditional oral culture to literate culture dominated by the printed word.[19] Universal education was a product of the printing press, and hence, education is centered on the major products of literate thought—namely, reading, writing, history, mathematics, and science.[20]

Enthusiasts note a contemporary transition of similar magnitude with the blossoming of new communication technologies: video, computers, the Internet, video conferencing, and so forth, all of which are merging into one large network that will reach anyone anywhere. Henry Jenkins describes how new media have triggered a "cultural convergence" that blends the roles of citizen with consumer and reshapes how people interact with entertainment, work, and learning.[21] More than just receivers of information, people are turning media into technologies of expression. The term *multimedia* is gradually being dissociated from *mass media*—we are expanding from simply "media by the few for the many" to "media by the many for the many."[22] Even though the mass media are becoming more centralized, the Internet media are becoming more diverse. People are gaining new voices and new ways of communicating with the world, as shown by the proliferation of blogs and social networking sites. These new media are likely to have as profound effects as printing, particularly on education, as we move into a digital culture.

Each of the new media has different affordances and constraints.[23] For example, video conveys sense and emotion more easily than text, but it is usually watched straight through, without stopping or going back, which makes it less amenable to study. On the other hand, computers support design and simulation in ways that text and video cannot. Enthusiasts assume that all of the different media will play a role in the design of learning environments. These different media can enhance learning by addressing the different learning styles and abilities of students and by using the media that are most appropriate for the material to be learned.[24]

Publication

Student work in schools has always faced the artificial barrier of being legitimate only within the confines of the classroom. When student work is seen only by teachers, students do not experience the authentic feedback that results from exposing their work to a real audience. In the case of initially learning a subject, insulating learning from external critique may make sense. But enthusiasts believe that as student work matures, students need opportunities to demonstrate their learning in legitimate contexts outside the classroom. The development of the Internet makes it possible for student work to become much more widely available to the rest of the world. The web is the first mass medium that has open access, so that anyone can publish his or her work in a place that potentially has a worldwide audience. This can provide a powerful motivation for students to produce substantial works that are meaningful to the community.

For example, YouthRadio.org is an award-winning site that provides an opportunity for youth to report on current events through new media. Youth Radio has trained thousands of underserved students in media-related production and careers, and provides a broadcast outlet for youth perspectives. The site includes user-generated election and political coverage, Google mash-ups that link current stories with geographic displays, reporting on significant events on the Internet (e.g., new viral YouTube.com videos), and audio feeds for three Youth Radio stations. The production aspect of new media allows for channels through which user-generated work can receive legitimate public exposure and scrutiny. Youth Radio stories are heard by millions of listeners each year through National Public Radio, iTunes, CNN.com, and the YouthRadio.org site.

As another example, in an Internet-based environment called the MUSE, which stands for Multi-User Simulation Environment, a college student who visited the Amazon rain forest returned to build a simulated rain forest that others could explore. Everything in the MUSE is done in text, so that the elaborate depictions of the rain forest are all verbal descriptions. It is like an adventure game, where you go down different paths, encounter different animals, and take various actions to affect the world. In another MUSE project, fifth-graders created a historical museum, where you might meet different presidents, such as George Washington, Thomas Jefferson, and

Abraham Lincoln. The presidents would tell visitors their thoughts on different topics, culled from their writings. The students produced an environment that anybody could explore by going into the MUSE over the Internet.

Enthusiasts argue that the Internet offers many different venues for communicating with the world. Students can send emails to other students and adults around the world. They can participate in chat rooms and communities that have participants from many different locations. A main motivation for participation in blogging or social networking sites is the opportunity to publish a representation of yourself that others will see. Constructing representations of your thoughts, preferences, and creativity allows others to identify you as a possible friend, or can open you up to criticism from those who do not share your tastes. In either case, participants learn about what they really think, and gain self-awareness from publishing public representations of themselves.

These different venues provide a reason to communicate with people outside one's immediate sphere, and so they provide a meaningful purpose for reading and writing, and developing multimedia presentations. Although security issues have limited the ability of some schools to make student work public, enthusiasts point to how technologies create access to external audiences that can provide legitimate contexts for students to learn from how others perceive their work.

Since students are leading the way in developing new models of communication, enthusiasts argue that it makes sense to let students take the lead in integrating new technologies into schools. School designs that foster interest-based communities in schools can motivate student learning by applying their skills to new areas of investigation. Integrating social networking sites such as MySpace or Facebook into the schooling process, or adapting online gaming to school content, could introduce the technologies students live with outside schools into the world of schooling. Enthusiasts argue that the presence of such technologies would push schools in the direction of embracing the liberating possibilities of new media rather than limiting their use through acceptable use policies.

Reflection

Reflection occurs when learners look back on their performance in a situation and compare their performance with some set of standards or with other performances, such as their own previous performances and those of experts. Reflection has received much attention as a vital aspect of the learning process for both children and adults. Donald Schön shows how systematic reflection on practice is critical for many professionals engaged in complex activities.[25] Designers of learning environments build supports for reflection into tasks by asking students to discuss and reflect upon the strategies used to guide their actions. Reflection can highlight the critical aspects of a performance and encourage learners to think about what makes for a good performance and how they might improve in the future.

There are three forms that reflection can take, all of which are enhanced by technology: 1) reflection on your process, 2) comparison of your performance with the performance of experts, and 3) comparison of your performance with a set of criteria for evaluating performances.

- Reflection on your process: Because technology makes it possible to record performances, people can look back at how they did a task. This allows them to reflect on the quality of their decisions and think about how to do better next time.
- Comparison of your performance with the performance of experts: Some computer-based learning environments allow learners to compare their decisions in solving a complex problem to an expert solution, so that they can see how they might have done better.[26]
- Comparison of your performance with a set of criteria for evaluating performances: Computer systems can ask students to evaluate their progress with respect to a set of criteria that determine good performance. For example, Barbara White and John Frederiksen had students evaluate their performance on science projects using a set of eight criteria, such as depth of understanding and creativity. These students improved much more than students who carried out the same tasks but did not reflect on their performance in the same way.[27]

Enthusiasts believe that technology creates real opportunities for students to improve their performance over time by building opportunity for reflection into learning environments. Using technologies that track student work makes looking back on their performance much more feasible.

THE ENTHUSIASTS' VISION OF SCHOOLING

In the enthusiast's view, computer-based environments promise a revolution in schooling of the same magnitude as the revolution in our culture set in motion by the Industrial Revolution. Technology enthusiasts favor a constructive approach to learning, where students, rather than teachers, do most of the work.

In his classic book *Mindstorms*, Seymour Papert describes the Samba schools that come together in preparation for Mardi Gras in Rio de Janeiro as a metaphor for what school should become.[28] Whole communities, including adults and children, work together for months to build floats and prepare elaborate entertainments. The children help the adults in whatever tasks need doing. There is much learning going on, both among children and adults, where the more expert teach the less expert how to do various tasks. It is apprenticeship in its most benign form, since everyone involved has a common goal to please the viewers of their floats and to win in the competitions. It is this vision of learning, but in a technology-rich environment, that Papert would like to see realized in schools.

In the technology enthusiasts' view, schools would look more like technology-rich workplaces. Students would work together on meaningful tasks with the aid of powerful computer tools. Many of these tasks would take them into the community. They might design and construct bike paths, investigate water pollution in local lakes and streams, build and update web pages for businesses, develop programming for community cable television, or do planning for the town using Geographic Information System (GIS) tools.

Interactive learning environments would also provide contexts where students could tackle real-world problems beyond the scope of the projects they can carry out in the community. They could put together news broadcasts about current events, analyze DNA sequences to look for genetic diseases, develop an animation of how bodies move in space in order to teach Newton's laws to other students, and so forth. In short, technology can provide the support for students to tackle complex problems, which would be beyond the capability of most students, not to say most teachers.

A major motivation for many technology enthusiasts is their unhappiness with current education. They subscribe to Dewey's notion that students should be actively engaged participants in learning, sharing their knowledge with one another rather than competing to get good grades. Like progressive reformers throughout the 20th century, technology advocates do not like the aspects of traditional school, where students are supposed to sit still and listen to teachers talk, memorize the information given them by teachers and books, and regurgitate that information back on tests. They think this destroys most students' curiosity and desire to learn.

In the technologists' view, such an education produces many more failures than successes. In fact, it is becoming clear that the students who do not do well in this highly competitive system will opt out of it in any way they can. While many progressive educators have attempted to change teaching and learning by using the conventional tools of curriculum redesign and teacher training, technology enthusiasts believe that computers can provide the kinds of immersive, customized, and adaptive learning opportunities that can reach the children who fail in schools. The challenge, from the enthusiasts' perspective, is to build technology into the core practices of school.

Technology enthusiasts envision schools where students are working on realistic tasks and adults play a supportive role to guide them to new activities and help them when they encounter problems. However, there is a long tradition of studying how and why efforts to change schooling have failed. Skeptics have argued that schools lack the resources, the training, the will, and the skill to change the fundamental practices of teaching and learning. Even with revolutionary tools like the new digital technologies, schools have stubbornly resisted changing what they do. In the next chapter, we turn to the skeptics of technology to understand the interplay between powerful technologies and school teaching and learning.

3

The Technology
Skeptics' Argument

For every researcher, teacher, and policymaker excited about the possibility of how information technologies can change education, there is a skeptic who questions the possibility or the value of technology in schools. Many people who have worked in and with schools note how the system stubbornly resists changes to its core practices. "It is not that schools never change. It's that schools change very slowly!"

The advent of computers in schools, argue the skeptics, carries the risk of either reducing the rich variety of classroom teaching and learning to the most predictable forms of rote learning or perverting the learning experience in the interests of commercial media. In either case, the conserving power of schools protects the core practices of teaching and learning from the distracting, or even dangerous, consequences of the new media.

Two leading technology enthusiasts, Dave Thornburg and David Dwyer, put together a set of quotes through the history of American education that characterize the resistance to new technology.[1] They reflect the way technology enthusiasts see the problems they are up against in reforming schools. They think that schools are always resistant to change, even when the change will clearly benefit students' learning. [2]

- From a principal's publication in 1815: "Students today depend on paper too much. They don't know how to write on a slate without getting chalk dust all over themselves. They can't clean a slate properly. What will they do when they run out of paper?"
- From the journal of the National Association of Teachers, 1907: "Students today depend too much upon ink. They don't know how to use a pen knife to sharpen a pencil. Pen and ink will never replace the pencil."

- From *Rural American Teacher*, 1928: "Students today depend upon store bought ink. They don't know how to make their own. When they run out of ink they will be unable to write words or ciphers until their next trip to the settlement. This is a sad commentary on modern education."
- From *PTA Gazette*, 1941: "Students today depend on these expensive fountain pens. They can no longer write with a straight pen and nib. We parents must not allow them to wallow in such luxury to the detriment of learning how to cope in the real business world which is not so extravagant."
- From *Federal Teachers*, 1950: "Ballpoint pens will be the ruin of education in our country. Students use these devices and then throw them away. The American values of thrift and frugality are being discarded. Businesses and banks will never allow such expensive luxuries."
- From a fourth-grade teacher in Apple Classroom of Tomorrow chronicles, 1987: "If students turn in papers they did on the computer, I require them to write them over in long hand because I don't believe they do the computer work on their own."
- From a science fair judge in Apple Classroom of Tomorrow chronicles, 1988: "Computers give students an unfair advantage. Therefore, students who used computers to analyze data or create displays will be eliminated from the science fair."

These points illustrate the long struggle educators have had with contemporary technologies. Rather than simply declare that "classroom wins," we consider this struggle a window for examining how and why schools have resisted past technologies, and whether the promise of the new technologies we discussed in Chapter 2 will face the same fate. The arguments from the leading skeptics profiled in this chapter suggest that the new technologies will never be central to schooling, just as earlier technologies, such as television, were never adopted in schools in the ways enthusiasts envisioned.

LOCKED IN PLACE?

There is a long history of technology enthusiasts predicting great revolutions in schooling as a result of technological innovations. Larry Cuban documents how radio, television, and filmstrips were all supposed to change schooling.[3] In each case, these innovations had little effect on the central practices of teaching and learning in schools. Now enthusiasts suggest that interactivity and customization make computing a fundamentally different kind of innovation from these earlier technologies. Yet, in a recent book, Cuban shows that computers have had little effect on teaching and learning in schools.[4] He argues that technological innovations that do not take the routines and organization of schools into account will have little effect on instruction. What is it about schools that make technologically driven innovation difficult?

Public schools are remarkably resilient institutions. In fact, the organization and proliferation of public schooling may well prove to be one of America's most valuable contributions to world culture. From a historical perspective, the tradition of government-sponsored mass schooling is a relatively recent phenomenon. While the state has provided educational opportunities for young children for nearly 2 centuries, the majority of adolescents did not graduate from high school until the 1940s.[5] The relatively recent origin of the public school system belies the degree to which the system remains receptive to changes. The American school system experienced a period of great innovation in the late 19th and early 20th century but has developed a stable structure since. Over this brief time, public schools have coalesced into a robust system that thrives in diverse environments.

This model of school has been variously called the "factory model" by Raymond Callahan, "real school" by Mary Heywood Metz, and the "one best system" by David Tyack.[6] The model organizes and governs schools at the classroom, school, and district level, and ties together instructional, curricular, assessment, and behavioral standards into a comprehensive package of practices and expectations.

At the basic level, schools are organized around classrooms of students at the same age. Each classroom typically includes a teacher and somewhere between 15 and 30 students. At the lower grades, one teacher usually guides students through all subjects. In upper grades, students move from classroom to classroom, so that teachers can specialize in their subject areas. In the typical school, the teacher is an expert whose job is to transmit that expertise to students through lecture, recitation, drill, and practice. The curriculum spells out what students are to learn and in what order. Although there is usually some effort made to customize and align curricula in individual schools, there is a remarkable and widespread agreement and expectations about what students learn when. Fourth-graders learn to divide fractions; high school juniors study the Great Depression. Testing is carried out in classrooms to determine whether students have learned what was covered, and if so they advance to the next grade, acquiring as they advance a record of courses taken and grades assigned.

The school system relies on common and well-tested technologies. The basic material tools for schooling are paper, pens, pencils, and chalk. Organizational technologies such as class scheduling, budgeting, grading, and matriculation practices enable the smooth flow of resources and people in and out of the schools. These tools are very adaptable to a wide range of community environments and well suited to the symbol manipulation, recitation, and recall involved in many curricula. The scope, sequence, and content of the curriculum are captured in the textbook, and worksheets provide versatile media for student interaction with content. Blackboards and overhead projectors provide cheap ways to support teacher explanations and sharing work. Though the ever-present loud-speaker system still interrupts classrooms with schoolwide announcements, overall school coordination relies heavily on paper for records and communication. While classes in science, home economics, and the arts rely on specialized technology, such as school laboratories, kitchens, and studios for their work, the majority of classroom instruction depends heavily on paper, pens, books, and chalk as the primary instructional media.

In each school and district, these features of the instructional system and their technologies weave together to form a complex system. As school systems have evolved, their components have developed mutual interdependencies. Over the years, the different components of the system have settled together to establish an equilibrium that reflects a balance among system components. For example, the generic technologies of classroom instruction lead to school designs that allow for teachers and students to move freely between classrooms. This, in turn, reinforces scheduling technologies that, with the exception of secondary science labs and vocational education classes, leave access to specific instructional technologies out of the process. The establishment of an equilibrium does not mean that the system stops moving. Rather, it means that the components of the system have achieved a balance, such that changes in the size of the student body or the location of the school are incorporated without changing the basic arrangement of system components. Once established, it is often difficult to move a complex system from its equilibrium.

The fit between practices results from many years of what Larry Cuban calls "situationally constrained choice."[7] Cuban argues that the choices available to teachers and leaders are constrained in terms of 1) school and classroom structures, and 2) a culture of teaching that arises in response to the stability of structures. These work together in his view to restrict the range of innovations realistically open to schools. The hard-won internal balance of system components provides a comfortable, well-tested environment for teaching and learning in many schools. Over time, this perception comes to be shared (and defended) by teachers, parents, students, and school leaders. Innovations that threaten the ways that curricula govern the yearly teaching plan or the tacit agreements between teachers and students in classrooms face a long, uphill battle for implementation. This is because when complex systems are in equilibrium, changing one part of the system usually results in other parts pushing back to restore the initial balance.

Jane David describes the interlocking and self-sustaining school system as a jigsaw puzzle.[8] Not only do the existing pieces depend on one another, but new pieces fit only into gaps and contours shaped by previous practices. For example, implementing a new mathematics curriculum pushes against the prevailing instructional, assessment, and curricular practices of schools. Teachers may lack the training or the will to change their instruction to fit the new curriculum, which may mean that greater numbers of students fail, resulting in parents clamoring to put back the old curriculum. The existing instructional system adapts to the new curriculum in predictable ways. Teachers can regard the new curriculum as a foreign invasion into their regular teaching practices, and try to fit it in with those practices. Even with professional development and monitoring, most teachers know that once in their classrooms, they can teach as they please. Hence, a highly evolved, complex institutional system can be locked in place and very difficult to change.

The technologies that guide a system can be as difficult to change as the practices they guide. Technologies that require a basic reconfiguration of instructional practice, such as radio or television, are marginalized to preserve school organizations based on text-based media. David Cohen argues that to the degree technology is flexible, it will be adapted to fit that system; to the degree it is not flexible, it will be ignored or relegated to the periphery.[9] Here, the plasticity of information technologies works against their power to change embedded institutional practices.

Although computers can open up new ways of teaching and learning, they can also be used to replace typewriters and file cabinets in schools dedicated to preserving a paper-and-text culture. Schools develop courses such as Keyboarding and Introduction to Computers not only to teach students new skills, but also to keep computers in their proper place. These courses tell students, "Computers can be useful, but you can learn all you need to know about them in one or two courses." Further, students who struggle to succeed in the traditional school program can be marginalized from peers through assignment to computer-aided instructional systems. Here, computers reinforce the message that new technologies are best used to ensure that the existing instructional system will not adapt to the needs of individual students.

WHY EDUCATION REFORMS FAIL

Schools have not been successful at teaching all children. Reformers have pushed schools to be more inclusive, more responsive, more challenging, and more accountable. A long tradition of educational reform movements have pushed schools to take on the role of becoming the primary vehicle for social and economic progress. These traditions of schooling and reform in America have grown up so closely interconnected that the history of schooling has become the history of school reform. However, while early on the basic organization of schools developed in response to reform efforts, lately many reformers have been frustrated with the seemingly stubborn refusal of schools to change.

David Cohen argues that the central reason why schooling is so difficult to change is the nature of the teaching and learning practices. He groups teaching with professions such as psychotherapy and nursing as a "practice of human improvement." These efforts all attempt to persuade clients to improve their own well-being by submitting to the established practices of the profession. Teaching is "living testimony to our faith that . . . [the] problems that have plagued humanity for time out of mind will yield to organized knowledge and skill."[10] Self-improvement is difficult, even under the best of circumstances.

Unfortunately, teaching in schools lacks the organizational support given to similar practices of human improvement. In schools, teachers rarely have a choice of clients, clients rarely have a choice of teachers, and clients are often unwilling to learn what teachers have to offer. As a result, teachers are reluctant to give up the hard-won gains that come from small victories in organizing teaching and learning. Such gains, often in the form of what Lee Shulman calls "pedagogical content knowledge," comprise the treasured practical wisdom of veteran teachers.[11] Hence, Cohen concludes that teaching is inevitably a conservative practice. When embedded in institutions that protect instruction from systematic change, a conservative practice is reinforced by a conserving institution. It is difficult for teachers to implement substantially changed programs when they already have dedicated years adapting to what the traditional system of school offers.

The organizational structure of schooling has developed three strategies for addressing innovative technologies without influencing the traditions of teaching and learning: condemning, co-opting, and marginalizing.

First, *condemn the technologies*. In the 1950s, for example, early developers of educational television promoted innovative programming to supplement existing K–12 schools. However, the American Federation of Teachers saw the new technologies as a threat to the existing investment in teacher expertise and stated that "we are unalterably opposed to mass education by television as a substitute for professional classroom techniques."[12] Media critics argued that there were good reasons for condemning the new technologies, in that they battle for the minds of students between learning and entertainment. Many schools have reacted primarily to the risks rather than to the potential of new technologies. Heirs to this spirit of prevention can be found in the appropriate-use policies of many schools that simply ban new technologies that are perceived as posing a risk to existing instructional practices.

Second, *co-opt the technologies* that support existing curricular outcomes and instructional organization and can be easily integrated into instructional programs. Drill and practice programs, such as *Math Blaster*, can be used to support existing math curricula. Similarly, lessons built into integrated learning systems, such as *Plato* (www.plato.com), reinforce the learning objectives of math, science, and social studies through curricula involving progressively more difficult, interactive learning opportunities. School systems with *Plato* can assign remedial help for students who struggle with traditional class materials to pass achievement tests.

Third, *marginalize the technologies*. Interested teachers can create innovative boutique programs alongside of the general school context where they can work with like-minded program advocates and students.[13] The high school (as well as universities and community colleges) have all grown through adding new boutique programs that extend the reach of the existing systems. It is relatively easy to add or remove separable elements of the system, such as adding computer courses or eliminating arts courses. However, reformers have not been able to change the very fabric of education where teachers pass on their expertise to students and then test the students to see whether they have learned their lessons. Reforms to build a more child-centered education have produced only minor changes, mainly in the more flexible domain of elementary education.

The contemporary demand for standardized curriculum and assessment in K–12 education makes adoption of new instructional directions based on information technologies even more unlikely. In most states, learning standards are keyed to both the development of basic skills and comprehensive coverage of disciplinary content. With accountability pressures rising in many schools, most efforts are going into practicing skills and covering required content. This emphasis on high-stakes measures of conventional skills and content does not encourage widespread innovation in teaching practice.

A conservative reliance on existing technologies works against rebuilding education around the kinds of skills for which computers and information networks provide an advantage in learning. In fact, Michael Russell and Walter Haney have shown that writing on computers actually leads to decreasing scores on pencil-and-paper writing tests, even when student writing improves as tested on computers.[14] This is because the process of writing on a computer is quite different from writing on paper. While the plasticity of information technologies can adapt to meeting a variety of learning needs, this very flexibility can create tools that work against the movement toward the more learner-centered focus in schools that technology enthusiasts advocate.

BARRIERS TO TECHNOLOGY USE IN SCHOOLS

While schools as organizations shape technological tools to serve existing instructional goals, there are also a variety of other barriers that act to prevent the use of technology in schools.

Cost and Access

Even though the costs of computers and network connections have declined considerably in recent years, cost is still a serious barrier to these technologies becoming central to schooling. Cathleen Norris and Elliot Soloway argue that for technology to make real inroads in instruction, the student to computer ratio in schools has to be 1:1.[15] Despite a considerable investment in computing infrastructure, the current ratio across the country is about five students per computer, and the ratio 9:1 in urban districts. This means that pervasive use of computers will still need to rely on home computers. There remains a considerable gap in home access to computers. By 2005, 89% of all Americans owned personal computers, and 68% of families with incomes below $25,000 owned computers.[16] But widespread access to computers and other digital devices has narrowed the gap between black and white Americans. A 2008 survey comparing Internet access between black and white Americans found that 68% of African Americans are online, compared with 71% of white Americans, and that 90% of African-American teens are online.[17]

For computers to become as central to schools as they are to workplaces, students would have to do most of their work in networked computer environments, including both class work and homework. But that would involve enormous expenditure to provide computers to every student. This would either require that each student have a personal laptop they carry with them wherever they go, or that there be enough computers in every room and home for each student to have a computer when they do their work. Otherwise, computers will be kept in laboratories, with perhaps a few computers in each classroom. In that case, most of the work students do will be offline, and computers will only be used for high-priority tasks, such as typing papers and learning how to do computer programming.

In addition to the high cost of purchasing machines are the high costs of maintenance and software. There has to be technical staff on the premises, who can fix basic problems with machines and network connections when things break. There also must be technical support people who can help teachers and students deal with loading new software onto machines and who can handle problems that arise when the teachers and students try to use new software. Students often know more about advanced information technologies than teachers and technology workers in schools. This knowledge gap means that technology support people must be continuously trained both to provide access to students and to protect the technology from students.

In recent years, the costs of providing computer security have spiraled. The relatively limited security precautions taken make many school districts appetizing targets for hacker activity from both inside and outside the school. And the cost of site licenses for software and software upgrades can be quite expensive. While businesses must invest in these facilities to remain competitive, schools have had difficulty justifying the increasing investments in upgrading software, maintenance, and security.

Classroom Management

Even classrooms that have computer resources present problems for instruction. David Cohen points out that since whole class instruction predominates in schools, putting computers in a classroom causes difficult management problems.[18] The teacher can have a few students work on the computers at one time, while working with the other students, but that can cause discipline problems, and the teacher must be comfortable splitting the class into different work groups. The kinds of individualized learning afforded by computers can disrupt the group instruction common in many classrooms. If the students at the computers are working together, they make noise that disturbs the other students. Students who do not get to work at the computers often feel left out. Most traditional classrooms simply do not have space for more than a few desktop machines, and the resources necessary to redesign instructional space are already scarce. Although laptops would solve the space problem, concerns about theft and breakage militate against their use. Putting computers in labs makes managing the machines easier, but may not help teachers and teaching. Bringing students to the lab means leaving class materials behind and competing for time with other classrooms.

In addition to the space problems, there are time and instructional problems in working with computers. Most K–12 class periods are only 45 to 50 minutes long. The start-up costs of working with computers, such as time to get the software installed and started up and getting students situated, pressure the teacher to cut into teaching time. Taking students to the computer lab takes more time. And unless the tasks are short ones, such as drill and practice systems provide, it is difficult to get much done in the time allotted.

A major incentive operating in schools is the demand on teachers to keep control of their classroom and maintain an atmosphere of quiet learning and study. Teachers are often judged on how well they keep control of their classrooms, and failure to maintain control continues to be a leading cause for young teachers to leave the profession. When students are working on computers, particularly when they are working in groups, there tends to be a lot of interaction and noise with students sharing ideas and helping one another. So it is difficult to maintain the quiet that teachers and administrators expect. This makes using computers seem risky to most teachers.

What Computers Can't Teach

Neil Postman makes a persuasive argument about the limitations of computers that captures much of what educators believe. This viewpoint provides a major barrier to computers becoming dominant in schools. Postman cites Robert Fulghum's *All I Really Need to Know I Learned in Kindergarten* for a number of lessons we all must learn as we grow up: "Share everything, play fair, don't hit people, put things back where you found them, clean up your own mess, wash your hands before you eat and, of course, flush."[19] He could have added many other kinds of knowledge, such as listening, expressing yourself clearly and forcefully, and obeying adults in authority. These are all things children will never learn from computers. And, as he points out, these are skills we spend many years learning, and school is where we learn most of them.

Teachers bring many things to learning that computers can never match. The best teachers inspire their students to believe in themselves and to work hard to accomplish their goals. They open up possibilities that parents and children may never see. They challenge learners' prior beliefs and encourage them to consider alternative ways to believe and to act. In the educators' view, computers are mere dispensers of content, and content is not the most important thing to learn as children grow up. Hence, most teachers and principals feel that computers should never dominate the classroom.

Challenges to Instruction

The innovative instruction that drives many computer applications also makes the teacher's job more difficult. Just as with other ambitious curricula, using computers in the classroom requires teachers to put extra time into gathering materials together and robs them of their conventional strategies to keep track of what students are doing. Challenging curricula also tax teachers' expertise, forcing them to test out untried ideas, often with unwilling students.

For example, David Cohen describes the fate of the new science curricula that were developed in the 1950s and 1960s by leading American

scientists and educators.[20] The goals of the new curricula were to emphasize understanding, thinking, and hands-on activities. But they ran into
difficulties because they departed from the standard school science curricula. Many teachers did not understand the new materials very well and
taught by rote, telling students what to do at each step. It was much more
difficult to teach with the new curricula, since teachers had to keep track
of all the materials and know how to deal with the issues and problems
that arose in working with the materials. The College Board had to develop
new tests to assess what the students in these curricula had learned, which
they abandoned after about 10 years. These kinds of problems are intensi-
fied when dealing with an uncooperative, mysterious technology. Given
the time and knowledge demands already experienced by teachers, it is
not surprising that most teachers do not want to deal with the additional
challenges introduced by computers.

Authority and Teaching

Computers act to dilute the authority that teachers have in classrooms—
especially the authority over what constitutes legitimate knowledge. When
connected to the Internet, computers open classrooms to a wide variety
of information from many different sources. In a conventional school, a
teacher controls the official information flow of the classroom. Because
computers provide access to more information than they can possibly
master, teachers risk losing authority by integrating computers into their
teaching. Teachers earn the respect of students in part from their knowledge and wisdom, and in part from their ability to engage and stimulate
their students. To the degree that students are getting their knowledge from
computer learning environments rather than from the teacher, it takes away
from the respect and authority that teachers would gain from sharing their
expertise with students.

Furthermore, to the degree that students are engaged with computers,
the teacher is not engaging their attention. David Dwyer and his colleagues
report a difficulty that many of their teachers feel when they allow students
to work on computers in computer-rich classrooms.[21] They seem to feel
guilty that they are not teaching the students, and they feel nervous about
all the talking and sharing of information among the students. Teachers
like to share their expertise. Were they to use computers extensively, they
would have to give up center stage. Most would not feel that they were
doing what they were trained to do—that is, passing on their expertise to

students. There are strong institutional and professional pressures that make giving up this control feel like a dereliction of duty. A teacher who acts as a facilitator can still form strong bonds with students, which will earn their appreciation. But by becoming facilitators rather than instructors, are they still teaching?

There is a general feeling that teachers have been losing authority over students in recent years. James Rosenbaum often asks today's students whether they have ever seen a teacher cry. Almost all have done so, even though 30 years ago, most students never saw a teacher cry. He argues that this is in part because school grades have no effect on students' success at finding jobs, or getting into most colleges. Of course, there is stiff competition among top students to get into elite colleges, but it turns out that most state colleges and community colleges only require a high school diploma, and most employers do not think that high school grades matter. So, unless students plan to go to an elite college, they have little incentive to please their teachers.[22] But, television, radio, and film also provide sources of information for students that make them question what teachers tell them and tend to downgrade the image of teachers. Taken together with peer interaction, the media help to reinforce a peer culture that offers an alternative measure of social value and authority in schools that supplants the authority of teachers. Teachers need this authority in order to justify why schoolwork is important for students to succeed in life. Computers can only serve to undermine their authority further.

Assessment

Standardized tests constrain how computers might be able to change learning in schools. The emphasis on high-stakes accountability testing across the country places a premium on how well students are prepared in mathematics and reading, and to a lesser extent, in science and social studies. So a lot of effort is spent on students practicing the reading and computing skills needed for these tests. Drill and practice software can fit with this kind of curriculum. But there is little room in the curriculum for adventurous uses of computers, such as to carry out in-depth research or complete meaningful projects. The standards movement across America is, in fact, working against the kinds of learning that computers facilitate best.

The skeptics argue that the prevailing organization of resources, routines, and expectations work together to thwart the substantial changes in teaching and learning promised by computers. In the traditional view, learning consists largely of memorizing essential facts and concepts, and performing procedures until they are automatic. The practices we cited above, such as the lecture and recitation methods of teaching, and testing for acquisition of facts, concepts, and procedures, are manifestations of this underlying societal belief about the nature of education. Only a small minority of educators hold the belief that education should be about students constructing their own understanding using computer tools.

The skeptics argue that in schools, the transformative power of technology will be co-opted by the ways schools have worked. David Cohen suggests that computer programs that support the current organization are most likely to be taken up by schools.[23] In fact, the exploding private market for assessment systems and data warehouses serves to reinforce the current conservative approach to standardized instruction. Thus, drill and practice programs, rather than more adventurous uses of computers, are the ones that schools tend to adopt. But they stay in the periphery of the school, such as computer labs, where the teacher can take students to practice the skills they will need for the many tests they must pass.

SYNTHESIS: INCOMPATIBILITIES BETWEEN SCHOOLS AND TECHNOLOGY

In this section, we contrast the hope of the enthusiasts with the caution of the skeptics. Enthusiasts have emphasized the transformative power of digital media, while skeptics have argued that computers have had minimal effects on schools and are not likely to be widely adopted in schools anytime soon. In our own view, this is because there are deep incompatibilities between the practices of schools and the imperatives of the new technologies. Below, we contrast the ways that schooling and the new technologies seem to be at odds with each other. These incompatibilities make it very unlikely that technology will have a large impact on schools in the foreseeable future.

Uniform Learning Versus Customization

Deeply ingrained in the structure of schooling is a mass-production notion of uniform learning. This belief stipulates that everyone should learn the same things. Despite the practices of innovations, such as special education, typical school courses are still structured so that everyone studies the same texts and has to pass the same examinations. This notion extends beyond the individual course to the notion of a set of required courses that extends up to graduate school. The notion that everyone must come through the process meeting a set of common requirements is very deeply ingrained in the notion of school.

But one of the great advantages that technology brings to education is customization. Computers can respond to the particular interests and difficulties that learners have. If you want to learn about Chinese history or the stock market, you can find lots of information on the web. Sometimes you may even find individualized tutoring programs to help you learn. As computers spread throughout society and the web becomes still richer with tools and information, education should move beyond the lockstep of required courses and basic skills. But to do this it has to go outside of the school where uniform learning is woven into the very fabric of daily practice.

Teacher as Expert Versus Diverse Knowledge Sources

Schooling is built on the notion that the teacher is an expert, whose job is to pass on his or her expertise to students. The legitimacy of traditional classroom instruction rests on the teacher's expertise as the source of legitimate knowledge. For many years, teacher education has focused on providing teachers with disciplinary knowledge and on the methods to teach this knowledge in classrooms. Textbooks are written to support these kinds of knowledge-based teacher expertise, because they serve to define the scope of information that students are expected to learn and teachers are responsible for teaching. This notion of teacher expertise is central to the enterprise of schooling.

In contrast, digital media provide ready access to many different sources of expertise. Video offers a variety of films and programs that present different worldviews. Before the advent of television and cinema, parents and teachers could prevail over children based on their much wider knowledge of the world. But as Neil Postman documents, that authority has been greatly diminished by what children are learning from television.[24] Computers and networks exacerbate the problem even more. Soon children will be able to download all the videos and music and written materials they want into their bedrooms. In a recent report, the Kaiser Foundation documents how far this trend has gone, with teenagers often living in an entirely different media space from their parents, and, of course, their teachers.[25]

Standardized High-Stakes Assessment Versus Specialization

The assessment technology that is employed in evaluating students uses multiple-choice and short-answer items, in order to provide objective scoring. But this form of testing requires that every student learn the same thing. The standards movement in the United States is leading to an expansion of high-stakes testing using objective methods. Standardized assessments are motivated by the reform effort to ensure that all children are at least educated to a common expectation for learning. However, standardized approaches to instruction, by definition, restrict the range of acceptable practice. There is less and less leeway for teachers to allow students to choose unique directions to pursue topics deeply, because this will not help them on standardized tests. And so our assessment system is leading us away from any kind of specialization by students in their learning.

To the degree that technology encourages students to go off in their own direction, it is in direct conflict with the standardized assessments pervading schools. So it is in the interest of schools to strictly limit the use of computers and networks to those activities that support students in doing well on standardized tests. But those are the least adventurous uses of computers, and they do not tap the computer power that enthusiasts proclaim.

Owning Knowledge Versus Mobilizing Outside Resources

There is a deep belief among teachers and parents that to truly learn something, it is critical to do it on your own without any reliance on outside resources. Therefore, when tests are given, students are usually not allowed to use books or calculators, much less computers or the web. Tests are administered individually to students, rather than having them work in groups. In fact, students are usually discouraged from working together in school and sharing ideas. It is deeply embedded in school culture that sharing and using outside resources is cheating. That is why it was such a revelation when Uri Treisman and Robert Fullilove, who were in charge of student affairs for minority students at the University of California, Berkeley, looked at Asian-American student performance in schools.[26] They found that a large part of the success of many Asian-American students came from the practice of studying together for courses and exams. This led them to set up study groups among students who struggled with their courses, which in turn led to substantial improvements in how they did at Berkeley.

The opposite is true of life outside school, where technology supports people in their use of outside resources. In the workplace, you are often judged on how well you can mobilize resources to accomplish some task. Knowing where to go for information or help is often the key to the successful completion of a task. The web makes accessing resources and help much easier. Many people also look up information about issues they face, such as medical problems, in order to make informed decisions. Technology undermines the need to know things yourself, as long as you know how to find the information and help you are seeking. Hence, technology and school culture are at odds as to what it means to know and do.

Coverage Versus the Knowledge Explosion

School pursues the goal of covering all the important knowledge that people might need in the rest of their life. As knowledge has grown exponentially, textbooks have grown fatter and fatter. It has become more difficult to cover all the important material, and so curricula have become "a mile wide and an inch deep." Experts from different fields decide what should go into each curriculum, and they are in competition with each other to include the topics they deem important. The easiest way to accommodate their ideas is just to add more and more to the sum of what students are supposed to learn.

Given the explosion of knowledge, people simply cannot learn in school all they will need to know in later life. Successful adults have learned how to find the information and resources they need to supplement their existing knowledge. In an age of technology, they exploit the web to find the information and tools to accomplish meaningful tasks. Not only do they need to be able to find information and tools, but they also need to know how to integrate information from different sources, to evaluate the reliability of those sources, and to use the powerful computer tools available to them to analyze the information and present it to others. But these form a learning agenda that is at odds with the school agenda of covering all the important material needed for later life. School cannot take on both agendas, since the curriculum is already crowded with the material deemed important for students to learn.

Learning by Assimilation Versus Learning by Doing

Deeply embedded in the culture of schooling is the notion that students should read, listen to, and absorb a large body of facts, concepts, procedures, theories, beliefs, and works of art and science that have accumulated over the centuries. An educated person is one who understands and appreciates these great intellectual products of human history. This view of learning comes to us from liberal arts education. It is our highest ideal of a cultured person, and so has very high status as a goal of education.

In contrast, the kind of education that technology fosters is a more hands-on, activity-based education. Computers are highly interactive and provide the learner with a wide assortment of computer tools to accomplish meaningful tasks. Hence, they are much more aligned with the "learning by doing" view of education than with the "assimilation of cultural knowledge" view of education that permeates schooling. The two views are not entirely incompatible, since it is certainly possible to embed much of the accumulated cultural wisdom into interactive learning environments, but it is not a natural fit. So technology is likely to take education in a different direction, toward design and construction of artifacts and analysis of complex problems and situations. This is a vastly different view of education from that which pervades the culture of schooling.

THE SKEPTICS' VISION OF SCHOOLING

Skeptics argue that schools will not change in the face of new technologies. The school system has become locked in place, making it difficult to change the core practices without disturbing the current equilibrium. So the skeptics feel that new technology, although it will be adopted for the library or media center and for tech prep and computer science courses, is not likely to penetrate the core of schooling.

Their vision of schooling in any case does not center on technology. They think the important goals of schooling are to inspire students to understand the great products of human thought, think deeply about issues, consider different viewpoints, present their views in compelling and coherent fashion, and so on. And they do not see technology as central to attaining these goals. In fact, many see technology as a distraction.

Schooling itself is conservative. Educators value the idea that everyone should acquire basic skills and deep disciplinary knowledge. Hence, they want to focus the schools on teaching the important knowledge that society has accumulated over the course of history, rather than the fads of the latest technology innovations. As a practice of human improvement, teachers work under difficult conditions and come to value the hard-found strategies that lead to student learning. Protecting what they know leads many teachers to suspect what might be left out with the promise of transformed practices. Further, there are many barriers to computer use in school, such as the problems it raises for classroom management and the authority of the teacher.

One way to think about the difference between the goals of schooling and the goals of technology is captured by a catch phrase: *School fosters just-in-case learning while technology fosters just-in-time learning*. Schools are designed to teach us everything we might need to know in later life. But perhaps this is a fool's errand, given the knowledge explosion our society has enjoyed in recent years.

New technologies, on the other hand, support an entirely different approach to learning. Learn what you need when you need it. What will it take for our society to change its concept of what it means to be educated? In the next two chapters, we look at the revolution that education went through from an apprenticeship-based system to a school-based system, and the revolution we are currently going through toward a lifelong-learning system.

4

The Development of American Schooling

There are many reasons why school as an institution hasn't accommodated new technology, as the skeptics argue. But, as the enthusiasts argue, technology is becoming central to all of life. We think this means that school will become less and less important as a venue for education. The historical identification of schools and learning will begin to erode as other legitimate venues for learning develop, first for adults, then for K–12 children. Such a systemic transformation of education is not unique in history.

There was a transformation in education in the first half of the 19th century much like the one we are experiencing now, from a system based on apprenticeship to universal schooling. In this chapter, we examine this transformation as a precursor to the current transformation. Just as the Industrial Revolution led to the development of universal schooling, we believe the Knowledge Revolution is leading to a new era of lifelong learning.

The Industrial Revolution brought people out of domestic and craft industries into factories. The overwhelming majority of people were farmers (about 90%) before the Industrial Revolution. In America, the Industrial Revolution brought many immigrants to the country and led to the rapid growth of cities. Horace Mann argued that education was needed for social cohesion, to give the new immigrants a common language and understanding of American democracy. He saw education as providing the means for everyone to become successful.

FROM APPRENTICESHIP TO UNIVERSAL SCHOOLING

Although a formal education system has long been recognized as a mark of a civilized society, early forays into organized education, such as the Greek

49

gymnasium, the medieval university, and the English grammar school, were restricted to a few elite students for a relatively short amount of time. When it came to practical skills, such as how to grow crops, make clothes, or produce goods, apprenticeship dominated the educational landscape.

Until the 19th century, education was largely the responsibility of parents. Most people were farmers, and children learned the skills they needed, whether it was reading and counting or plowing and sewing, from their parents or other kin. This was an apprenticeship system, where individual children were taught all they needed to know by those close to them. Where people took up other occupations, such as crafts or midwifery, apprenticeship was the way they learned these occupations. Often, they were apprenticed to a friend or relative of the family, if not to their parents. They learned by observation, imitation, and guided practice. As Lawrence Cremin states, "In general, the pedagogy of household education was the pedagogy of apprenticeship, that is a relentless round of imitation, explanation, and trial and error. In addition a small proportion of households provided systematic tutoring and regular communal devotion."[1]

In early 19th-century New England, Horace Mann led a movement toward universal schooling that shifted the responsibility of educating children from the family to the state. Although many primary and grammar schools sprouted up in America before the 1830s, in large part the responsibility for education belonged mainly to the family. The early American system reflected the English model. Cremin describes the English system as follows: "Most English youngsters did not go to school at all; those who did went principally to what was euphemistically called a petty school (or dame school), where they studied reading and writing for a year or two under an indifferently prepared instructor. A small proportion, made up entirely of boys, might attend a local grammar school, where, if they stayed the course over 6 or 7 years, they might develop considerable facility in Latin, along with a modest knowledge of Greek and Hebrew."[2] It was this English system that was largely replicated in the American colonies.

The question this chapter addresses is why the transformation from apprenticeship to universal schooling took place and how it developed over time. Our thesis is that the American school system resulted from a chain of events that included: 1) the invention of the printing press, 2) the Reformation, 3) the American Revolution, and 4) the Industrial Revolution. The last of these was the precipitating event that caused the push for universal schooling among a group of humanitarians concerned with the welfare of children in an industrial society. We will briefly describe the role of the first three precursors in leading to the transformation and then describe how the Industrial Revolution changed America, bringing about in its wake the development of universal schooling. Then we will describe how schools evolved over the course of the first 100 years of universal schooling.

Invention of the Printing Press

The invention of the printing press led to widespread development and diffusion of knowledge. As more and more knowledge accumulated, there was a continual increase in what children needed to learn to succeed in the adult world.

A number of writers have tried to characterize the shift that occurred with the invention of the printing press as society moved from traditional oral culture to literate culture dominated by the printed word. As Walter Ong argues, old people were revered in oral cultures because they were the storehouses of memory, whereas written records came to replace this role of old people in literate cultures.[3] Similarly, Ong argues that "study" became possible only when there were written records. Writing down ideas makes them easier to evaluate and challenge, and thus to be modified and refined over time. This was critical to the development of science. Bruno Latour argues that it was the invention of "immutable mobiles" such as books and maps that was critical to the development of science. His term, *immutable mobiles*, emphasizes the permanence of the records and their distribution.[4] Universal schooling was ultimately a product of the printing press, and hence, education is centered on the major products of literate thought—namely reading, writing, history, mathematics, and science.

The Reformation

Elizabeth Eisenstein argues that the invention of printing brought on the Protestant Reformation.[5] Both Luther and Calvin advocated that an accessible Bible would allow Christians to evaluate Catholic doctrine for themselves. Bibles only became widely available in vernacular languages, such as German and English, with the invention of printing. One of Luther's great contributions was the translation of the Bible into German. This advocacy of reading among the Protestants then was an early movement toward the primacy of individually acquired knowledge over the authority of tradition. Together with the scientific revolution, the Protestant Reformation marked a watershed change in the status of knowledge, creating a need for new educational institutions designed to facilitate the growth of knowledge outside the clergy.

This Reformation spirit made an early imprint in American history. The Massachusetts Puritans, who were followers of Calvin, passed a law in 1642, just 22 years after the landing of the *Mayflower*, which dictated that parents were responsible for their children's education. The law asserted the state's right to ensure that every child was educated. It made education compulsory, but made no provision for schools or for teachers. The teachers were to be the parents or private tutors. Every family was responsible for the religious and moral upbringing of their children under pain of a fine.[6]

The initial spark for the movement to universal schooling was provided as early as the Massachusetts Act of 1647, which required that towns of 50 families or more had to hire a schoolmaster for the children. The act outlined a complete system of popular education. The law called for every township of 50 families to appoint one of their number to teach all children to read and write, and for every township of 100 families to set up a grammar school to instruct youth to be fitted for the university. But there was little uniformity in the education that children received. Some towns were very conscientious, but others were not. The pressure exerted on the towns by the colonial government fostered the development of education in Massachusetts.[7]

Maris Vinovskis sees the enactment of these early school laws as "a reflection of the attempts to promulgate correct religious views and to overcome the growing indifference of many families to religion and home education."[8] The laws reflect a general growth of schooling in colonial America, and particularly in New England. Taxpayers were reluctant to pay for education, and towns frequently reaffirmed parents' responsibility for educating their children. Yet, once schools were established, parents were quite willing to send their children to these schools, rather than teaching them at home.[9]

The American Revolution

The Enlightenment carried the democratization of knowledge started by the Reformation into the political realm. The establishment of a new country provided the founders with an opportunity to chart new institutions to serve the public good. In an essay, Benjamin Franklin called on a generation that had "received a good education in Europe" to now turn its attention to building similar, if more practically oriented, institutions in the colonies.[10] Thomas Jefferson's views on education flowed from his commitment to the "natural rights of man." The capacity of each person to exercise these natural rights required a government that was responsive to the desires of the populace, which in turn required a strong education system to help citizens understand and be able to defend their rights. America was the first government to embody many of the principles of the Enlightenment in practice. Critical to the development of universal schooling was the contentious decision to spread voting rights in America beyond the class of property owners to every male, with the exception of slaves.

Lawrence Cremin characterizes American education before the revolution as follows: Most children were taught via apprenticeship whatever skills they needed for the work they would do. Well under half were likely to have had any formal schooling, though there were some New England towns in which schooling was virtually universal. Two themes emerge: first, the centrality of the household in all childhood education and most later education, particularly for women, and second, the role of self-education for men and even more so for women.[11] Even though the colonies were beginning to develop an educational agenda, parents were still responsible for education.

Cremin writes that after the revolution, "It was increasingly argued that if there was to be universal exercise of the rights of suffrage and citizenship, all of society would have to be educated to this task."[12] Even before the Constitution was drafted, the Northwest Ordinance of 1787 declared that "schools and the means of education shall forever be encouraged" and the Land Ordinance of 1785 provided for the public finance of schools in newly organized territories and states.[13]

As George Washington said in his farewell address, "Promote then as an object of primary importance, institutions for the general diffusion of knowledge. In proportion as the structure of government gives force to public opinion, it is essential that public opinion should be enlightened."[14] In advocating the Bill for the More General Diffusion of Knowledge in the Virginia legislature in the 1780s, Jefferson wrote to his friend George Wythe, "Preach, my dear sir, a crusade against ignorance; establish and improve the law for educating the common people. Let our countrymen know . . . that the tax which will be paid for this purpose is not more than the thousandth part of what will be paid to kings, priests and nobles who will rise up among us if we leave the people in ignorance."[15] The law never passed the legislature, but 50 years later, many of its provisions came into practice.

Although Federalist leaders, such as Alexander Hamilton, were hesitant about relying on popular education as a condition for political power, many Republican leaders, such as Thomas Jefferson, were strong advocates for an educated populace. They argued that while monarchies needed an education that would prepare people for their proper place in the social order, republics needed an education that would prepare people to make wise policy decisions and motivate them to choose public over private interest.[16] This call for an educated populace was not realized immediately, but it formed the basis for the movement toward universal schooling in the 19th century.

The Industrial Revolution

In America, the move toward universal schooling originated in New England and was spread by persuasive leaders such as Horace Mann, John Joseph Hughes, and Catherine Beecher. The Industrial Revolution, however, turned the universal schooling movement from an evangelical movement to a practical necessity. In America, the Industrial Revolution not only attracted citizens from the farms to the cities, but it also fueled one of the most dramatic immigration waves in history. The application of industrial technologies to agriculture both produced the food necessary for rapid population growth and reduced the numbers of people necessary to produce it. David Tyack notes that "urbanization proceeded at a faster rate between 1820 and 1860 than in any other period of American history." For example, in a single year, 1847, Boston added more than 37,000 Irish immigrants to its population of 114,000.[17]

Frederick Carlton argued that there were only three possible ways to occupy children in the cities: 1) working in factories, 2) getting into trouble in the streets, and 3) learning in schools.[18] Once child labor laws were enacted, the choice between education and crime became clear to urban leaders. Horace Mann argued that education was needed for social cohesion, to give the new immigrants a common language and understanding of American democracy.

Horace Mann became superintendent of schools in Massachusetts in 1837. He led a movement of humanitarian reformers who were concerned about the fate of children in an industrial society. Mann made many public arguments as to how education was the means to make every person a wealthy and successful contributor to the new nation. He was particularly concerned about preparing the many new immigrants with the values and skills needed by the new republic. As Carlton argues, these leaders saw the existing evils of child and female labor, juvenile crime, and unemployment, and they glorified the desirable features of the earlier form of domestic industry, with its intimate personal relations between workers and employers. They joined hands with the labor movement to advance the cause of tax-supported schools. Educational progress was most marked in the cities where these two forces developed their greatest strength.[19]

State-provided schools signaled a shift away from the family with respect to responsibility for education. This shift did not go unopposed. Property owners, who paid the majority of the taxes, often opposed state-supported schools. This was particularly true of land-owning farmers who did not experience the urban problems of crime and poverty, and thought the only purpose of education was to prepare children for a successful life on the farm. Farm families, therefore, felt that they could provide all the education their children needed, and so in general, rural areas were opposed to tax-supported schools. These parents reflected the beliefs of colonial Americans who "stressed the importance of educating and catechizing their children at home."[20]

But after the onset of the Industrial Revolution, "nineteenth-century parents assumed that learning to read and write would occur in a classroom."[21] This signals the shift that occurred in education, from a family responsibility to a state responsibility. This shift came to permeate the thinking of Americans, leading ultimately to the belief that education occurs in school, and is largely missing from the rest of life. Urban citizens turned to the expansion of schooling, often at little cost to themselves, to address the problems of juvenile delinquency and competition from child labor in growing cities. In the end, it was the fact that the burgeoning urban population could vote in the new American republic that made it possible for the new educational institutions to prevail against the rural populations.

Most people today assume that universal schooling will always be with us, but of course, most people in the 17th and 18th centuries probably assumed that apprenticeship would always be the dominant form of learning. Though long dormant, the view that education might best occur in the home, the community, and the workplace rather than in the school is beginning to emerge once again.

THE ESTABLISHMENT OF UNIVERSAL SCHOOLING
IN AMERICA

In the era of apprenticeship, when children went to school they attended small, one-room schoolhouses where they would learn to read, write, and count, supplemented by a little religion. The early years of universal schooling saw many developments in the ways that schools were structured and operated—that is, there was extensive invention of new ways to do things. As the system evolved, it became more and more locked in place: The elements of the new design of schooling evolved together into a coherent system to meet the demands of a democratic and growing society. But as the system became more rigid, it ceased to evolve as the society around it continued to evolve, and so in recent years, it has become more and more out of sync with the demands of a continually evolving society.

Our focus is not on the story of how the American school system developed, but rather on how the system moved from a period of experimentation and invention to a stable system that is difficult to change. This stability mirrors the stability in the apprenticeship system that was only overcome as a result of strong economic, social, and political forces. We think this is an inevitable pattern with any institution, as the arguments of the economist Mancur Olson make clear.[22] In their youth, institutions are looking for ways to deal with different aspects of their environment, and so they experiment with different structures and strategies. Those that are successful stick and form part of the environment into which new structures and strategies must fit. Thus, a system evolves where the pieces fit together, and where there are established strategies for maintaining the organizational structure when faced with changes in the outside world. Then change becomes very difficult, except under the extreme pressure of possible extinction.

In the colonial years, the towns and villages set up independent one-room schoolhouses. They were largely ungraded and the teachers were males. As schooling became more common and America became a more populous and urban society, the school population grew very quickly. So the old model of the one-room schoolhouse had to give way. Some of the first innovations were to develop graded schools, where students had to pass examinations to move onto the next grade. There was also a movement, though it was hotly disputed, to recruit teachers from the ranks of women. At the same time, there was an attempt to make teaching a profession, as an occupation for a lifetime, rather than the practice that was common in the early years, where young women would teach until they married. As part of the professionalization of teaching, normal schools to prepare teachers were established, the first in Lexington, Massachusetts, by Horace Mann in 1837.

The evolution that was to take place can be seen from David Tyack's characterization of the schools in Boston in the first half of the 19th century. Public education in Boston in the mid-1840s seemed to reformers more like a collection of village schools than a coherent system. Responsibility was diffuse, teachers had considerable autonomy in their decentralized domains, and the flow of information was erratic and insufficiently focused for purposes of policy. The primary schools, founded to prepare children to enter the grammar schools, were mostly one-room, one-teacher schools scattered across the city.[23]

Tyack goes on to describe how a Boston educator named John Philbrick convinced the Boston school board that the schools required a new kind of building—one which has since been dubbed the "egg-crate school." In 1848, Philbrick became principal of the new Quincy School. The building was four stories high, with a large auditorium for 700 pupils and 12 classrooms, each of which would accommodate 56 students. Every teacher was female and had a separate classroom for the one grade she taught. The students were divided into classes based on tests, and all the students in a class studied the same subjects. According to Tyack "Thus was stamped on mid-century America not only the graded school, but also the pedagogical harem. This system caught on fast."[24]

Tyack describes the problem faced in Chicago at mid-century: "year after year thousands of children could not attend school for lack of seats. In 1860, 123 teachers faced a staggering total of 14,000 scholars in their classrooms. Indeed, the pressure of numbers was a main reason for the bureaucratization that gradually replaced the older decentralized village pattern of schooling."[25]

In the latter half of the 19th century, there was a move to establish public universities. The first public universities were established in Michigan and Wisconsin in the first half of the century, but the movement expanded greatly after 1862 when the Morrill Act was passed, providing funds to establish land-grant universities, where agricultural science was to be pursued. Public colleges and universities were one of the great inventions of American education, and have played a profound role in the development of America itself.

A leader in the second stage of the education movement was William Torrey Harris, who became superintendent of the public schools in St. Louis from 1868 to 1880 and U.S. commissioner of education from 1889 to 1906. He emphasized discipline and a curriculum centered on the "five windows of the soul"—mathematics, geography, literature and art, grammar, and history. In St. Louis, he was faced with thousands of children entering the school and too few teachers and classrooms. "Harris's answer was the graded school, organized by years and quarter-years of work, with pupils moving through on the basis of regular and frequent examination."[26]

Education for small children was integrated into the system in the second half of the century. Margarethe Shurz, a follower of the German educator and psychologist Friedrich Froebel, opened the first public kindergarten in America in Watertown, Wisconsin in 1856. By 1900, there were more than 4,500 kindergartens all over the United States. William Torrey Harris embraced the kindergarten as a part of the school curriculum with his K-8-4 (kindergarten, 8 years of elementary school, and 4 years of high school) plan for American schooling.[27]

High school provided another key piece of the system. As commissioner of education in 1892, Harris organized a group of leading educators into the Committee of Ten, charged with establishing a high school curriculum. With the exception of Latin and Greek, the core courses that the Committee of Ten established make up the bulk of the academic high school curriculum today. These courses were organized in what came to be known as Carnegie units. As David Tyack and Larry Cuban describe, in 1906, the president of the Carnegie Foundation defined a "unit" as "a course of five periods weekly throughout the academic year" in secondary school subjects. These "periods" came to be about 50 to 55 minutes long. This academic accounting device has been so firmly established that every attempt to dislodge it has been unsuccessful.[28]

An established physical organization of school was also rounding into shape. In 1910, William A. Wirt, who was superintendent of the Gary, Indiana, schools, invented a new system for efficiently running a school, which he called the "platoon school." The plan was arranged so that all of the rooms were in constant use. "For example, while one group was in its home room receiving instruction in reading, writing, and arithmetic, another group was in the music room, another in the shop, another on the playground, etc. When the bell rang, the students would shift to the next class."[29] This formed the basis for the organization of today's high school.

Other features of the contemporary educational landscape also began to take place shortly after the turn of the 20th century. At the 1904 National Educators Association (NEA) conference, Margaret Haley spoke about the need for teachers to organize and join the labor movement. At the same time, Elwood Cubberley, dean of the Stanford School of Education from 1917 until 1933, called for redesigning schools on the model of the modern bureaucratic organization. Tyack described how the move to state-sponsored schooling led to new educational institutions requiring a professional class of certified leaders and teachers to develop and maintain bureaucratic structures.[30] Part of organizing meant developing a system of "continuous measurement of production to see if it is according to specifications."[31]

This emphasis on measurement was fueled by the emergence of a strong statistical assessment movement led by educational psychologist Edward L. Thorndike. A pioneer in using statistics to measure learning, Thorndike stated that "we are no longer satisfied with vague arguments about what this or that system of administration or method of teaching does, but demand exact measurements of the achievement of any system or method or person."[32] Soon statistical measures were developed to assess intelligence, learning, efficiency, teaching, and leadership. These measures, in turn, reinforced the bureaucratic organization of school management and further isolated teachers from administrators.

Many characteristics of the school system now in place were innovations made in the initial years. There were other innovations that came in after these: the consolidation of rural schools, the development of the middle school and the community college, the adoption of widespread tracking in the schools, the provision of special education services, and of course, the development of the Scholastic Aptitude Test (SAT) for college admission. But since 1920, it has become much more difficult to make changes in a very stable system. As Tyack and Cuban argue, "The basic grammar of schooling, like the shape of classrooms, has remained remarkably stable over the decades. Little has changed in the ways that schools divide time and space, classify students and allocate them to classrooms, splinter knowledge into 'subjects,' and award grades and 'credits' as evidence of learning."[33] They argue further that this grammar of schooling has frustrated generations of reformers who have tried to improve the schools.

Tyack and Cuban go on to say, "The grammar of schooling is a product of history, not some primordial creation. It results from efforts of groups to win support for their definitions of problems and their proposed solutions. . . . Reforms that enter on the ground floor of major institutional changes, such as the rapid expansion of elementary education in the nineteenth century or the differentiation of secondary schools in the twentieth, have a good chance of becoming part of the standardized template."[34] The evolution of schooling from innovative practices to a stable system of school organizations follows Mancur Olson's argument that the accumulation of regulations and practices over time leads to mature, but rigid, institutions.[35]

THE EVOLUTION OF A SCHOOL SYSTEM

The school structures and institutions that evolved in the first 100 years of universal schooling solved a set of problems facing a growing and urbanizing country in very efficient and effective ways. The solution that was arrived at may not have been the only possible solution, but it did deal with the problems America faced in creating a system of universal schooling. Our argument in this section is designed to show how various pieces of the system were natural solutions to the problems faced in constructing a system of universal schooling and how these solutions became integrated over time into an interlocking system of universal schooling.

- *Compulsory attendance* was the main thrust of universal schooling. The new American republic faced the problem of a largely uneducated population and many new immigrants. The goal of compulsory attendance was to ensure that the populace was educated enough to make wise political decisions, since the control of the government in this new republic had been turned over to the people. There was a further goal to provide the entire population with the skills and knowledge needed to be productive workers, so that the nation as a whole would prosper. And finally, Horace Mann felt that compulsory attendance would gradually help provide students with the skills and knowledge to overcome the initial conditions of their lives. Compulsory attendance started with the younger ages but was gradually increased to 16 years as the country felt the need for education expanding.
- *Graded schools* were a response to the problems created by the huge increase in students brought on by compulsory attendance and a large influx of immigrants. Grouping students of the same age and experience together made it much easier for teachers to address the needs of their students. They could teach the same lessons to all the students at the same time. They could address the questions and problems that arose for the class as a whole. They could assess students on the same materials. Graded schools eased the burden

on teachers. Working with students of the same age reduced the amount of curricular knowledge for teachers and made it easier to control classes. Later, the widespread use of tracking in the schools made classes of students even more homogeneous.

- *Tests* were introduced in order to make it possible to sort students into classes where all the students had roughly the same ability. They were then used to track the progress of students through the system, so that they would advance to the next grade based on demonstrating that they had mastered the material covered in the current grade. Thus, tests were essential to the goal of maintaining homogeneity among the students in each class. They further served to define what the students were expected to learn and soon were used by teachers to motivate recalcitrant students to do the work, so that they would not be held back a grade. So tests came to perform a number of essential functions that were necessary to sustain a universal schooling system.

- *Textbooks* were introduced to solve the problem of determining what the students should learn—i.e., they served to define what should be covered in the curriculum. This was necessary to provide some uniformity in what students were learning in the different schools across the country. Particularly in the early years, one of the major purposes of textbooks was to provide teachers with knowledge of what they were supposed to teach. Many teachers were not professionally trained in the 1800s, and so textbooks specified for them what information to cover. Even today, many teachers rely on teachers' editions of textbooks to help them learn the material that they are to teach and guide them in how to present the material to students.

- *Carnegie units* addressed the problem of uniformity across a very diverse country. By specifying what courses should cover, they allow students to move from one school to another with some coordination in what the students learn. In particular, it allows colleges and universities to determine what students have studied in high school and whether they have been adequately prepared to take on a course of study in college. In a highly mobile society, such as America, the kind of coordination provided by Carnegie units is essential to placing students when they change schools.

- *Comprehensive high schools* allowed schools to offer a diversity of courses to suit different kinds of students. In the beginning of the 20th century, high schools provided the additional years needed to teach all the new knowledge and skills that have accumulated since the Industrial Revolution. In order to accommodate this new information, the years of schooling have steadily expanded and now for most students include years beyond high school. High school also served to keep youth out of the workforce, which gave labor unions more leverage to raise the wages of industrial and service workers. The growth of knowledge led to fatter textbooks and extended schooling, but these accommodations are reaching an upper limit. In comprehensive high schools, some students could follow an academic track in preparation for college. Other students could take courses that emphasize preparation for work. Sprawling comprehensive schools provided the model for the "shopping mall high schools" that aimed to provide all things for all students.[36] High school staffs grew beyond teachers to include guidance counselors, social workers, vocational educators, security officers, and food services. The comprehensive school was the solution to the problem of how to meet the learning needs of a wide variety of students.

These features of the current school system were natural solutions to the problems of constructing a universal system to educate a diverse population. The system that evolved has proved very effective in educating a highly diverse population. But the society has continued to change, while these features have been locked in place for over 50 years. So the pressures are building for new solutions to the problems of education.

HOW THE DEMANDS ON SCHOOLS HAVE CHANGED

By the 21st century, we have seen great technological and social changes that have yet to be reflected in the schools. Previously, the school system evolved to adapt to incremental changes in the community and the curriculum, often simply by adding programs, teachers, and buildings to the existing schools. This means that while the conditions under which the schools operate changed, the school system has been quite stable. Now, however, the changes in technologies are producing increasing tensions for schools. Schools are expected to prepare students for a different world, and public policies hold schools accountable for making progress. Schools scramble to meet these accountability requirements set by national and state governments while teaching more and more students from diverse cultural and language backgrounds. We think that the demands on schools are creating the conditions for radical change, like the one that occurred in the mid-1800s, when the current system of education evolved.

The technological changes in society have accelerated some of the most profound influences on schools. The pervasiveness of television and other new media helped produce a youth culture that is increasingly complex and sophisticated—what might be called the "adultification" of youth. The peer culture that has come to dominate students' lives is often hostile to school learning. Schools struggle to address the excesses of an autonomous peer culture in schools. For example, a recent survey from the National Center for Education Statistics (NCES) found that in 2005–2006, 24% of public schools reported that student bullying was a daily or weekly problem.[37] Another NCES survey found that the major reason parents chose to home school their children was their concern about the environment of the schools, such as safety, drugs, or negative peer pressure.[38] Schools try to respond to these social issues by developing new programs while at the same time making classroom instruction more engaging.

Three demographic changes have also led to changing pressures on schools: 1) the increase in the life span, 2) the decline in the birthrate, and 3) the increasing diversity of the American population. The aging population and the declining birthrate have meant that a smaller proportion of the adult population has children in school. This makes it increasingly difficult to tax the general population to pay for schools. Further, the opening of other occupations to women has meant that schools have had increasing difficulty in attracting the best and brightest women to a traditionally female-dominated profession.

The increasing diversity of the population has meant that it is often more difficult to use the same instructional strategies to teach students from different backgrounds. Immigration created very diverse urban schools in the late 19th and early 20th centuries, but the demands have changed for educating minority students for a knowledge economy. This renewed diversity in the public schools has provoked demands to reduce the achievement gaps among African-American, Latin-American, Asian-American, and Euro-American students. Policymakers and parents have turned to schools as the central institution to reduce the achievement gap and to provide food and basic social services, including medical and psychological counseling. Diversity increases pressure on schools to individualize education to address the needs, desires, and abilities of different groups within the population.

Along with the political and social pressures of racial and ethnic diversity, religious groups have also pressed for a schooling system that reflects their values. Evangelical Christians, orthodox Jews, both black and Near Eastern Muslims, and Catholics have expressed concerns about teaching children moral values and beliefs grounded in faith communities. At the same time, the separation of church and state and the identification of morality with religious belief among many Americans has led most public schools to shy away from explicitly teaching morality. Hence, religious groups have begun to turn away from public schooling altogether and toward using learning technologies for their children through home schooling.[39]

A higher level of affluence in the American economy has fueled the ability of many parents to use technologies to customize education for their children. The increasing wealth in society has led more and more people to pay for their own educational services. This has meant increasing numbers of people paying for private schools,[40] buying computers and network services for their children, paying for tutoring, buying books and educational toys and games, and taking courses in community colleges or adult education programs. At the same time, corporations and other organizations are spending more on training for their employees. Altogether, these trends have led to a steady increase in private spending on education in recent years.

The exponential growth of knowledge has also put increasing stress on the schools. It is said that there are as many scientists, researchers, and authors alive today as lived in human history up through 1950. Educators appear to feel that much of this new knowledge must be taught to students to prepare them as citizens to make public policy decisions, and as workers to fulfill the increasing need for technical expertise in the workforce. School curricula organized around content coverage have coped with the knowledge explosion with fatter textbooks, faster coverage of topics, developing extensive content standards, and extending the years of schooling.

Finally, the technological revolution we are currently going through has all the ramifications for the education system that we detailed in the initial chapters. In particular, there is more and more demand for people to be thinkers and lifelong learners, since technology is rapidly replacing people in the routine jobs of the society. Functioning effectively in society requires people to be able to use a variety of technologies to accomplish sophisticated tasks. This means that there is enormous pressure on education to move away from the traditional goals of memorizing facts and learning to carry out routines. The schools as they are currently constituted are preparing people to live in the last century rather than the new century.

THE CYCLE OF REVOLUTION

As we've discussed, the demise of the apprenticeship system in favor of universal schooling as the form of education we know today was precipitated by a number of seemingly unrelated movements. The printing press led to a flowering of knowledge that children must acquire to survive in the world. The Reformation leaders pushed for everyone to learn to read, so that people could learn what the Bible says for themselves. The American Revolution made an educated population necessary so that the people would make wise political decisions. And finally, the Industrial Revolution destroyed old patterns of living and working, forcing Americans to develop a new system for educating youth in the modern world. These events culminated in the universal schooling system, which took many years to evolve.

There were many innovations that were introduced over the first 100 years of universal schooling. These innovations evolved into a strong system that addressed many of the problems of educating a diverse American population. But as the system evolved, it became much more resistant to further innovation. The schools, therefore, have become more and more out of sync with the rapidly evolving technological society around them today. Something about education will have to change. In the next chapter, we consider all the different ways that education is changing outside of the schools.

5

The Seeds of a New System
of Education

The history of American schooling was marked by an early flexibility that has since coalesced into a system that is "locked in place" and unable to adapt to new conditions. How will schools be able to respond to the new technologies that have changed the face of work and everyday life?

Schools as we know them will not disappear anytime soon. Schools were prevalent in the era of apprenticeship, and they will be prevalent in whatever new system of education comes into being. But the seeds of a new system are beginning to emerge, and they are already beginning to erode the identification of learning with schooling. As these new technologically driven seeds germinate, education will occur in many different, more adaptive venues, and schools will have a narrower role in learning.

The different parts of our school system came together to meet the demands of a young country in the midst of an immigration explosion and an industrial revolution. Once developed, the institutional structures of schooling have remained fairly constant over the last 90 years. But the society surrounding the schools has experienced constant change.

The seeds of a new education system can be seen in the explosive growth of home schooling, workplace learning, distance education, adult education, learning centers, educational television and videos, computer-based learning software, technical certifications, and Internet cafés. Many of these seeds will affect the learning of children, but many others will affect people of all ages, as learning becomes a lifelong enterprise. The face of education is changing rapidly, and it remains to be seen exactly what form it will take. But we can explore some of the possibilities by looking at these new developments.

HOME SCHOOLING

Home schooling has been burgeoning in America over the last 25 years. Based on a survey in 2003, the U. S. Department of Education estimated there were 1.1 million children being home schooled, and that the number had increased by 29% in 4 years.[1] The total enrollment is similar to enrollments in Georgia or New Jersey, which have the 9th- and 10th-largest school enrollments. The survey found that about 2.5% of two-parent families and 1.5% of one-parent families engage in home schooling. The survey also found that 21% of the families engaged in home schooling hired a tutor for their kids and 41% used some form of distance learning. It is a larger movement than the charter school movement, which only about 1.2% of students attend, and it is growing steadily.[2]

Home schooling has been successful at improving student learning. Children who are schooled at home score significantly better on standardized tests in every subject area.[3] Overall, they score in the 87th percentile, near the top of the range (0–100) of their peers. They do about equally well whether their parents are certified as teachers or not. And unlike public schooling, home-schooled children's scores on these tests do not depend on the education level of their parents. Home schooling also reduces differences in scores related to race and gender. These data suggest that almost all of the differences due to student background, typically found among students in public schools, are eliminated by home schooling.[4] We can only imagine that this is due to the fact that parents who do home schooling care deeply about their children's learning.

The recent widespread focus on home schooling started with the educator John Holt, a liberal writer who became disillusioned with the rigidity of schools.[5] These early arguments emphasized how home schools could encourage kids to pursue the topics they care about most and take responsibility for their own learning. But it was the Christian home-school movement in the United States that fought the legal battles in the 1980s to make home schooling possible across the country. Christian home schooling advocates were concerned about what they thought the public schools left out: moral values. By educating their children at home, Christian home schoolers felt they could instill the kinds of beliefs and values that they believed kids should acquire. The home-schooling movement has grown rapidly over the last 30 years among both liberals and conservatives. Currently, there are two large associations of home schoolers, one conservative and one liberal, each emphasizing different values.[6]

Both conservative and liberal proponents of home schooling agree that the family is the appropriate institution for education. Also, both home-schooling groups are concerned about peer pressures in the schools, feel their children will learn more at home, and believe children will not develop the consumerist and anti-intellectual values of the peer culture. And they worry about violence in schools. It may turn out that other religious, cultural, and political groups will push to develop materials and support groups to foster home schooling for their communities. So, for example, Muslim Americans, Mexican Americans, libertarians, and Mormons, among others, could devote resources to developing home schooling that emphasizes their beliefs and values. Such movements may further fracture the cohesiveness of society, as we discuss later in Chapter 7.

A possible future trend is for home schooling to become a mass movement if parents pool resources and begin to mix a variety of strategies for providing education for their children. Even the most diligent home-schooling parents only spend about 3 or 4 hours a day working with their children.[7] There is a variety of strategies that home schooling might use that do not involve the parents, such as kids taking specific classes at a school or college or from a local service provider, participating in activities organized by home-schooling groups, and taking online courses. At the same time, groups of home schoolers might come together in homes or churches to share the parents' supervisory burden. Sharing supervision frees parents to work part-time and take 1 or 2 days a week to work with the group of children. They might even hire a retired teacher or professional, or even an older student to work with their children for a number of days each week. Although some of these strategies are expensive, the home-schooling movement has mostly been driven by people who are not wealthy.[8] Hence, there is a variety of ways for parents to reinvent education for their children.

Technological advances have fueled the development of home schooling, though they did not give rise to the movement. Internet curriculum materials help organize learning content, leaving parents and others to play the role of facilitators. In fact, William Bennett, formerly secretary of education in the Reagan administration, worked to develop K12.com in order to provide computer-based curriculum materials for home schooling. Virtual charter schools, such as Florida Virtual Schools, provide some of the administrative and curricular structures to support home schooling through distance education. As we argued earlier, technology fits much more comfortably into the home environment than into the school environment.

Parents of home schoolers may, in fact, be more helpful than teachers in a context where the content of what students are learning is embodied in computer- and video-based materials. Teachers view themselves as experts, whose role is to convey their knowledge to students. In contrast, parents do not think of themselves as experts and, hence, they take on the role of a coach more naturally. The role of coach puts more responsibility for learning onto the student. The parents are there to help the student figure things out and to encourage the students to work hard, but they usually do not take on the role of explaining everything to the learners. Figuring things out for themselves becomes a major job for home-schooled kids.

In about 10% of families that do home schooling, the mother works outside the home. This provides a considerable contrast with the 85% of American families with working single parents or married parents who both work. Will only a small proportion of the population be able to home school their children? This is an open question, but it seems worthwhile to consider whether it is possible for home schooling to become a much larger movement, encompassing a substantial proportion of the school-age population. One problem is that many career jobs require more than 40 hours per week of work, and when people reduce their work to part-time status, they imperil their career advancement. Home schooling clearly requires at least one parent to spend time and effort to support children's education. This is a fundamental economic problem. Unless society finds a different balance between work and family, it seems unlikely that a large proportion of the population will engage in home schooling. But it does seem possible that the movement will grow to include 5% to 20% of the population.

We can illustrate how home schooling might look in the future, as it spreads to new segments of the population. Imagine a Mexican-American couple, Miguel and Rosa, with two young girls, Margarita and Maria, living in Los Angeles 5 to 10 years from today. Miguel works as a janitor in the evenings, and Rosa cleans houses during the day. They fear all the peer pressure that their daughters would face if they were to attend the Los Angeles schools. So they decide to home school the two girls, by joining a Mexican-American association that has put together a K–12 computer-based curriculum for Latino children. They buy an inexpensive computer for each of the girls, so they can download their lessons and access materials from the web. They know a high school girl in the neighborhood, Juanita, who gets good grades in school, and they hire her to come in 4 days a week after school from 3:00 to 6:00 P.M. to help the girls with their school work.

Juanita goes over their work with them in the afternoon, asking why they did different things and answering any questions that come up. Miguel and Rosa can't pay her a lot, but she feels that the extra money helps her buy clothes and that she learns a lot from teaching the two girls.

Miguel, the father, monitors the girls during the day, making sure they are working on their lessons and taking them to the YWCA for gym classes and to outings arranged by the Mexican-American association for home-schooled kids. The outings take them to places such as the Children's Museum, the LaBrea tar pits, and the Huntington Gardens, with guides who explain everything about the different sites. The kids on the outings range in age from 6 to 12 years old, and the girls become friends with several of the girls who come on the outings. At dinner, Rosa, the mother, asks the kids about what they are learning and encourages them to pursue topics in which they seem particularly interested, such as the difference between life in Mexico City and Los Angeles.

As you can see from this scenario, it is easy to imagine the possibilities for families to take up home schooling. Of course, the economic reality of parents who must work long hours to maintain their standard of living makes it difficult for parents to make such commitments to their children's education. But the advent of charter schools in many states makes it easier for groups with common beliefs to acquire public funds to organize their own virtual schools outside the K–12 mainstream schools. The incentives are there to avoid the dangers of traditional urban schools and to focus their children's learning around the values that the parents share. As technology-based curricula are developed and associations of home-schooling parents become widespread, it should be easier for parents to manage. And if it looks possible to do, many more people are likely to try it.

There are upsides and downsides to the spread of home schooling. It may indeed lead children and parents to take more responsibility for their education, but at the same time, it means that children will not be learning common content and values. E. D. Hirsch worries in his seminal book on cultural literacy about the loss of a common cultural understanding among Americans.[9] Home-schooled children are likely to pursue different topics that reflect their cultural values, and communication between different groups may become more difficult. Home schooling goes against the spirit that moved Horace Mann and his colleagues to advocate universal schooling in order to integrate people from diverse cultures to share common knowledge and values.

WORKPLACE LEARNING

Much of the discussion up to this point has addressed K–12 learning. However, we argue that innovations in workplace environments will soon influence learning throughout education. We can illustrate how learning in the workplace is developing with another vignette. Laura Hollander manages an ice cream store in California. The corporate web site has an online training game that teaches customer service by interacting with customers in an animated simulation. The virtual customers make requests and register complaints that the game player must handle to the customer's satisfaction. The simulation is fun to play and gives Laura lots of experience in dealing with novel situations. Such simulations are gradually reshaping how workplace learning happens across America, and the design of these simulations is influencing education across all age ranges.

Workplace learning has been rapidly expanding over the last 25 years as companies and the public sector have realized they need to continually re-educate their workers to handle complex equipment and solve novel problems. In part, these new training programs are aimed at preparing workers to handle new kinds of tasks and to use new tools. But corporations are also faced with remedial training needs for the kinds of knowledge and skills that students should learn in schools. To develop training programs, businesses sometimes work with colleges and a growing number of private firms that develop training programs for corporations. Learning in the workplace is becoming the new frontier for the next-generation learning environment. To illustrate the changing face of workplace learning, we will describe efforts by three large firms—Motorola, Accenture, and Xerox—to prepare employees for the changing world of work. We will also describe how the military is using simulation to enhance the training of recruits.

In the early 1980s, Motorola hired line workers who were reliable and willing to work hard. But during the 1980s, international competition forced Motorola to change its hiring and training practices. The company needed to have workers who took responsibility for the quality of their products and could make decisions using statistical analyses to ensure quality. In other words, Motorola needed thinkers rather than hard workers. But it found that many of its workers could not read or do simple computations, even though they had been good workers up to that time in Motorola's eyes. Because the company had always tried to inspire loyalty among its workers, it decided to invest in their education to provide them with the skills they needed to compete in the new world of manufacturing. In fact, the company's training and education budget went from $7 million to $120 million in the 1980s and has been growing ever since.[10]

In order to provide the training its workers needed, Motorola assigned William Wiggenhorn to develop a training program for all Motorola workers, from top management on down. He developed training to teach statistical process control and basic industrial problem solving. The new skills, however, did not result in new work practices. When workers would keep charts to track production statistically, nobody would ask to look at them. The managers took the courses, but they did not change their practices. So, after many false starts, top management started to enforce a concern for quality on the managers, and quality improved over 10-fold. But still Motorola needed to improve performance and reduce its management ranks in order to meet the intense competition. It decided that this would require workers with at least a seventh-grade level in reading and math. When the company saw the scope of the education problem, it began working with community colleges and technical institutes to offer both remedial reading and math courses, as well as technical and business skills, such as accounting and statistical control. Although the colleges sometimes had courses with the right titles, Motorola found that the courses often did not meet its real needs. So it began working with colleges, as it did with other suppliers, to design courses that met its needs. All these efforts led Motorola to cast its education programs as a new Motorola University.[11]

Accenture, one of the largest consulting firms in the world, also made a major effort in the 1990s to improve the education it provided for its employees.[12] In the 1990s, working with the Institute for the Learning Sciences at Northwestern University, Accenture developed a new approach to its training based on what are called "goal-based scenarios." In this approach, employees are given tasks that reflect the kinds of work they will have to do out in the field for their clients. For example, in one course, the employees had to design a user interface for a reservation system to meet a set of specifications that a fictional hotel chain required. The learners were divided into teams of four that were competing to produce the best design. Senior managers played the roles of executives for the client and coaches for the teams. The teams were provided with extensive online documentation and worked out their designs in an online environment. There were sessions at the end of each day where they would reflect with their coach on the day's progress and what they should try to do next. It was a challenging environment, in which they were learning by doing rather than by listening. Although they did not collect pre- and post-data to see how much students learned, employees rated the course as much more successful than employees had rated the previous lecture and discussion course.[13]

Accenture developed a whole series of these training exercises for employees at different levels, which cost over a million dollars per exercise to develop. It also developed a number of CD-ROM-based exercises that it could ship to offices around the world. For example, one of these, designed for managers, trains them to be good coaches by putting them in an advisory role to a design group that is having problems working together effectively. The CD-ROM exercises incorporate many of the same features as the goal-based scenarios they encounter in their training program, such as reflection sessions and advice from senior partners, which is recorded on video. The kind of training systems that Accenture develops are expensive to build, and there are no specific data on how effective they are. However, Accenture feels that these courses teach the practical knowledge and skills its employees will need to succeed, which its previous lecture-based courses had failed to do.[14]

Workplace learning has also transformed how some companies decide what counts as professional knowledge. For example, Xerox had a large facility in Leesburg, Virginia, where technical representatives learn to diagnose and repair copy machines. The company has developed extensive documentation that links particular types of machine failures to the actions that the tech reps are supposed to follow to fix the machines. Unfortunately, many copier problems fall outside the domain of these manuals, and when they do, the tech reps may spend hours trying to find what is wrong and fix it. The tech reps learned to cope with these problems by sharing war stories over lunch or coffee. They talked about the times when the manual was no help, and how they figured out what to do. The stories provided an informal education for the other tech reps as to what to do when they have similar problems. By telling their stories, the tech reps formed a kind of teaching and learning community. Xerox eventually realized that the stories were a valuable resource, and so it created an online repository for the stories, called Eureka. The tech reps are proud to add their stories to the system, because a good story adds to their reputation for skill and ingenuity. Xerox has managed to create a computer-based learning system that is actually used and provides useful information to tech reps throughout the company.[15]

The military has spent billions of dollars developing simulations that put learners into virtual worlds where they practice the skills they will need to carry out their jobs. One such simulation provides the capability for trainees to drive tanks around a virtual terrain. The virtual tanks have all the capabilities of the real tanks the army deploys in battle. Different trainees can drive their individual tanks in formation across the virtual terrain, avoiding obstacles and figuring out how to navigate different terrain features, such as streams and gullies. As they go over a hill, they might encounter enemy virtual tanks driven by experts trained in enemy tactics. A simulated battle would ensue, and the trainees would have to use everything they have learned to outmaneuver the enemy tanks. After the battle, they replay the battle to reflect on what would have been the best tactics to use. This is a much less expensive way to train tank commanders than the army's traditional exercises. The simulation might be called "tanks but no tanks."

Recently, both the military and corporations have been building simulations around the most popular online video games, using the tools that have been developed for creating these games. The military, in particular, has used game design as a path for recruiting and training a generation that grew up on video games. While initial computer-based games proved valuable for teaching how to aim and shoot weapons, the next generation of games is increasingly designed for teaching technical and management skills such as resource allocation, collaboration, critical thinking, and tolerance for failure.

Companies have also picked up on the potential of games for training. Canon, for example, has developed a simulation where technicians must repair simulated copier machines that have different faults inserted in them. In one Cisco game, players must put together a computer network on Mars. The development of computer simulations to put learners into novel work environments is a fast-growing enterprise.

We can imagine a day when most of the training that workers get for their jobs bypasses traditional educational institutions and takes place in online environments. Salespeople might practice their skills with simulations of recalcitrant customers. Doctors might practice their skills by trying to diagnose unusual cases. Future travel agents might be challenged to develop cost-effective trip plans using the web. In fact, almost any job-related skill can be taught by practicing the skill, and computer simulations can create immersive environments where the target skills are necessary for solving engaging problems. More and more workplaces are investing in such simulations. It is likely that future workers will have to spend much of their time learning, as workplaces keep introducing new processes, techniques, and equipment. Workers may spend their whole lives learning in order to survive in a changing workplace.

DISTANCE EDUCATION

Consider another vignette: From her small public school in Medford, Oregon, Anita Sanchez teaches a poetry course with students from all over the country. It is a course that most students cannot find in their high school, and it gives them a chance to connect with other kids who have an interest in poetry. One of her students, Stacy Williams, has also been taking courses in Latin for 3 years from Colorado Online Learning, which she uses toward her high school degree in Colorado. It gives her a chance to pursue her interest in Latin much more deeply than she could hope to do in her high school. Colorado Online Learning is just one of many virtual schools offering courses to students around the world.

Distance education has, of course, been around for a long time. Correspondence courses and PBS programs such as *Sunrise Semester* have reached thousands of students over the past century. However, the Internet is pushing new kinds of interactive distance education at both the K–12 and collegiate level. The University of Phoenix, for example, is famous for having tens of thousands of online students all over the country. Leading universities, including Stanford, Harvard, and Carnegie-Mellon, offer a variety of courses to distant locations. The model of the Open University in the United Kingdom has spread across the globe. Venture capital firms have been investing millions of dollars to develop distance education. In addition, almost every state has developed virtual high schools to provide courses to students that are not offered in their own schools. Distance education has already spread widely, and it will inevitably keep growing in the coming decades.

The University of Phoenix is the most successful online university in America. It has more than 100,000 students altogether, including more than 30,000 online students.[16] It started as an academically oriented institution in 1976 on a for-profit basis, and was accredited by the North Central Association of Schools and Colleges in 1978. It aims its program at working adults who want to advance their careers, emphasizing courses in areas such as business, management, and information technology. Many of the students attend classes at learning centers in 22 different states.[17] Being in residence at a university has great advantages for students, such as developing social networks and participating in university life. Most people regard online degrees as quite inferior to degrees from brick and mortar universities, and it will be a great loss for young people if they miss out on "going away to college." But online institutions will continue to thrive for people who already have a job and simply want to advance their career.

The University of Phoenix started its online program in 1996, with an emphasis on attracting students who have specific career goals. The online classes are small, usually around eight students per class. The students often work in teams on projects, and hold asynchronous discussions online. This means that busy professionals can participate in the evening or on weekends, whenever they have time. Because the University of Phoenix is a for-profit institution, it is very concerned with customizing courses to meet the needs of its students. It conducts extensive surveys of students and carries out systematic evaluations of how much the students are learning. The university has found that online students learn as much as classroom students, and seem to like their courses about as well.[18] Whether online students do, in fact, learn as much in general as students who attend classes on site is an open question, but online courses tend to have higher dropout rates, which could bias results.

The Open University in Great Britain was one of the first distance education efforts to become widely successful. It currently has about 180,000 students and was rated the top university in England and Wales for student satisfaction in the 2005 and 2006 UK government national student satisfaction surveys.[19] It does not rely on online learning extensively; rather, it maintains learning centers in many British towns, where students can get help from tutors and take exams. Most of the courses use materials that are mailed to the students or are broadcast over television. It has become the largest university in Britain and the government likes it because it has the lowest per-pupil costs of any British university. More than 10,000 students with disabilities enroll in the Open University, because they do not have to travel extensively to attend. And, of course, working people find it easier to attend the Open University, because they can spend time flexibly taking courses. The Open University model has spread widely to other countries, and in fact, the Open Universities in India and Pakistan have enrollments in the hundreds of thousands.

In recent years, K–12 schools have begun to develop distance education. Distance education options range from providing niche and remedial courses for students across the country to full-fledged comprehensive school programs. Programs such as NovaNet provide advanced and remedial courses for districts with limited resources or for students who struggle with traditional school offerings. Virtual K–12 institutions help smaller schools offer a wide range of courses to compete with larger schools. Research suggests that small high schools may be more effective at building community between teachers and students, because the teachers come to know the students much better and can address their needs more effectively. In fact, the Bill and Melinda Gates Foundation has an initiative to foster the development of small schools, using technology resources that have been developed in recent years. Distance education gives small schools a way to compete with larger schools that offer a wide variety of courses.

Many states and districts are also experimenting with virtual high school programs, where teachers at different schools in the system offer online courses to students at other high schools in the state. Utah, with 35,000 online students, and Florida, with 21,000 online students, are farthest along on this path. In some cases, the virtual high schools are organized as charter schools that can enroll students from across the state. States such as Pennsylvania and Wisconsin are currently engaged in fierce debate about the equity issues involved as some districts lose students, and the funds that go with them, to the new virtual charters.

Distance education is a growing phenomenon. As busy people realize that they need more education, they increasingly opt to take distance education courses. Although distance education has a head start in adult education, the recent development of virtual K–12 schools will provide future challenges for the brick and mortar public schools.

ADULT EDUCATION

An 80-year-old retired bookkeeper we know leads an active intellectual life. She regularly takes trips around the world with Elderhostel to places such as Costa Rica and Egypt to learn about life in other cultures under the guidance of experts. She often goes on retreats to a college in Maine, where she spends a week walking and talking about the great books assigned under the tutelage of a professor at the college. And she takes literature courses at Brandeis University as part of their program for retired people. All this is in addition to participating actively in a book club.

She is very active intellectually, which is not so unusual among retired people today.

Adult education is growing rapidly as more and more adults take courses in adult education programs. In part, this is because people are living longer, healthier lives. The adult education movement is a manifestation of the new spirit of lifelong learning. Adult education pushes K–12 education to reconsider the goals of learning. From an adult education perspective, the goal of K–16 education is to create the skills necessary to participate in lifelong learning, rather than to aim at self-contained curricular goals. While many adults are returning to schools for undergraduate or graduate degrees, others now go on the web to learn about particular topics in which they are interested, such as how to invest in stocks. Book discussion groups are steadily increasing in number. Older people often go on vacations with an educational purpose, such as a trip to an interesting locale with an expert providing guidance.

In recent years, many towns in America have established adult education programs to meet the needs of this new generation of students. Cambridge, Massachusetts, for example, has two such programs—Cambridge Adult Education and Harvard Extension. Many professors like to teach in these programs because the students are so enthusiastic about learning and sharing their experiences. But many of the teachers are working practitioners, who have a particular specialty and an interest in teaching. The courses these programs offer vary widely, from interpreting James Joyce's *Ulysses* and Ingmar Bergman films to making pottery and photographs. Older adults, especially the growing number of retirees, flock to these courses. They seem more and more interested in extending their education.

The multiplication of book discussion groups is quite remarkable. Alongside the popularity of television, book sales have increased manyfold over the last 40 years, spurred on by the development of paperback books. But this growth is ending now with the development of the web. Still, people of all ages are joining groups that get together regularly to discuss a book they have all read. Usually, the groups decide to read current fiction, but the Great Books Clubs focus more on scientific and political literature. Some people even go off to college campuses in the summer for a week of discussion, where there are heavy reading assignments and beautiful surroundings.

At the same time, educational tours are proliferating. Public radio stations and colleges are getting heavily into this business. People can take an art trip to Italy to see the great masterpieces of Italian art, together with experts who explain the significance of the work and the history of the Renaissance. Or they can travel to Galapagos Islands with one of their favorite radio personalities, to see the many strange creatures native to the islands and learn about Darwin's development of evolutionary theory. Retirees are particularly attracted to these educational tours, and so they are expanding as the number of wealthy retirees increases.

Adult education is one of the major growth industries in America. Although much of the learning that goes on is recreational, it still provides valuable knowledge that sometimes may lead to a second career or the deep pursuit of a long-term interest, which was put aside for work at an earlier age. Perhaps it will turn out that some of our most productive citizens are the older people, who use their retirement leisure time to keep learning.

LEARNING CENTERS

Privately owned learning centers are growing to fill gaps in the existing education system. These are currently most common as preparation for taking national tests, such as the SAT and ACT, and to provide tutoring for children who are having problems in school. We also see learning centers beginning to develop for adult education. As with home schooling, this initial proliferation of learning centers relies on the family's ability to pay for additional educational services. We expect that learning centers will employ more and more network-based education and will spread as a way to obtain specific knowledge and credentials.

Princeton Review, Sylvan, Thompson, and Kaplan are only a few of the companies that provide learning centers. In fact, Sylvan is now one of the largest corporations in America. Some of these companies are setting up centers in towns and cities, where people can go to prepare for some kind of test or to get specialized teaching in some area of weakness. The federal No Child Left Behind Act requires failing schools to provide tutoring support for children. Private companies are popping up everywhere to address this new market. Philadelphia, for example, has hired Princeton Review to help teach children the math skills they will need to improve their test scores. This is likely to be a growing trend, where school districts hire companies to help students with skills that district schools need support to teach successfully.

Private vendors of education are very prominent in Japan already. Many Japanese families send their children to afterschool programs, or *jukus*, starting in middle school, that are designed to prepare children for college entrance exams. The colleges in Japan are ranked in prestige, and they base entry on the difficult nationwide exams that students take after they finish high school. Parents enroll their children in the jukus from an early age to give their children an edge in the college entrance race. The competitive race for prestigious colleges in America has led some parents to send their children to similar learning centers to improve chances of admission. If anything, the competition for college is likely to increase, and so parents may become more willing to buy an advantage for their children.

Learning centers are also making an impact on career education. In the 1990s, the U.S. Department of Education launched an initiative to support nonprofit community technology centers to serve communities where access to computers and other technologies is very limited. The community technology center network (http://www.ctcnet.org) now has more than 1,000 centers in many different locales, such as housing projects, storefronts, community organizations, and libraries. Most of the participants are minorities, and a large proportion are African-American and Hispanic women. They range in age from 13 to 91, half of them between 20 and 31 years of age, but with a large number of teenagers as well. Most come to learn job skills and take classes at the centers, as well as to use the Internet facilities. Many acquire improved English language skills, get tutoring and homework help, or participate in GED and other adult education programs. They also use computers to get information from the Internet, send and receive email, set up web pages, and carry out their own self-directed projects.

For example, one center in the poorest neighborhood in Cincinnati, called Media Bridges, offers free classes, as well as the means to create media productions. Media Bridges loans out equipment for free, library-style, including cameras, microphones, computers, and studios, so that people can create messages to take to the citizens of Cincinnati via Media Bridges' cable channels, Internet radio station, or web sites. One of their most active users, Derrick Blassingame, attended the virtual high school in Cincinnati at age 16 and appeared on *Larry King Live*. Derrick produced *Youth Speaks*, a show that provided a forum for young people to speak with other youth, as well as adults, about the issues that affect their lives. Media Bridges' free Internet terminals provided a place for Derrick to keep up on the latest issues affecting youth, while he did post-production work on *Youth Speaks*. Email was especially helpful, as it saved Derrick time and money when corresponding with those who work with him on problems, such as teen pregnancy or poverty.

We can imagine how learning centers might evolve as an alternative to school at the high school level and beyond. Teenagers and adults might go to the centers to study particular subjects that would be useful to them. For example, they might take online courses they need to get a high school diploma, to master English as a second language, or to acquire job skills they need to get a good position. The online courses can be graded in difficulty from novice to expert. The center would have a manager to help learners get started, to keep discipline, and to deal with problems that arise. It is also likely that some experienced teens and adults would be willing to help others who are having problems with the content or the technology. Everyone at the center would be focused on getting through their courses and taking online assessments associated with each course.

Such centers would produce an entirely different learning community from a school classroom. There would be no age segregation, and so the problems of youth culture would likely be lessened. Teens and adults would be working on their courses in parallel, as children did in the old one-room schoolhouses. There would not be any bells to tell learners when to start and stop. They would start work when they get there and stop when they are tired or come to a good break point. Learners would have a wide array of online resources available to help them as they work on their courses. The manager would administer online assessments when learners are ready, and a number of people could take the assessments at the same time. The problems that high schools face, such as violence and peer pressure, are not likely to arise in such a setting, if adults and kids are mixed together working on different lessons.

Learning centers, whether nonprofit or for-profit, are spreading widely. They usually offer classes, as well as providing access to technology. They are oriented toward obtaining specific knowledge and skills that the users want to obtain. We expect that learning centers will proliferate in the coming years. New learning center designs must be able to draw on public or shared resources to increase access for poor and disenfranchised students. They will have managers who can help out when learners have difficulties and who can administer tests when students are ready for them. They provide a new setting for learning, where many of the problems facing schools are mitigated.

EDUCATIONAL TELEVISION AND VIDEOS

The effects of television and video on learning have been widely criticized. Although many once praised television as a panacea, teachers and parents now often feel that television is largely responsible for students' unwillingness to sit still and listen in classrooms. Video is certainly a passive medium, compared to reading or interacting with computers and people. But it has had significant educational effects, some positive and some negative, over the last 40 years.

Since the start of Children's Television Workshop (CTW) in the late 1960s, there has been a proliferation of educational programming on television and videos for children. The impact of television on learning has been greatly expanded by two developments: 1) the growth of the public television network (PBS), and 2) the advent of cable television. PBS has turned over almost all of its daytime television schedule to children's programming, and together with CTW, has produced a variety of children's programs such as *Sesame Street*, the *Electric Company*, the *Muppet Show*, *3–2–1 Contact*, and *Barney*. These shows have been exposing young children from different backgrounds to some of the basic skills, such as phonics and counting skills, that they need to succeed in school and life.

Public television has also been producing a large number of shows for the education of adults. These are on topics that include science, nature, history, politics, art, music, and theater. Now, with the development of cable, there is a host of additional outlets for shows of these kinds, such as the Arts and Entertainment Network, the History Channel, the Learning Channel, the Discovery Channel, and all the current-events channels, such as CNN and C-SPAN. Even police and legal dramas are educational in a way, as illustrated by the story of Marcus Arnold, who became a legal expert on AskMe.com after watching legal shows on television (see Chapter 1).[20]

At the same time, there has been a proliferation of videos for kids that emphasize learning, which many toddlers watch over and over. These videos often feature kids' favorite television stars, such as the Wiggles and Dora the Explorer. Unfortunately, many shows, like *Dora*, are using product placements and advertisements to sell directly to the kids, putting commercial pressure on busy parents. For kids with a special passion, such as horses or dinosaurs, there are many videos that parents can buy, and they can become specialists on these topics before they can even read. Videos and television for young children provide an access to education that is an entirely new phenomenon. So many programs and videos have been produced in the last 30 years that many kids are now spending a lot of their time watching videos, rather than playing outside. It gives them knowledge they may find useful later in life, but at the cost of inactivity.

Neil Postman claims that television has had the dramatic effect of revealing adult secrets to children and turning education into entertainment. As he points out, millions of kids are watching adult shows, often late into the night. Thus, kids are learning about drugs, violence, incest, adultery, and so on from television or from other kids who watch television. He thinks this is leading to the disappearance of childhood. Kids were once protected from many of the social ills that adult society endures, but these protections have been breaking down in recent years. At the same time, he argues that shows like *Sesame Street* have taught kids that learning does not require hard work and concentration, but merely sitting back and watching things happen. This is a kind of education that kids are getting from television, though we might not like to see it happening.[21]

In his provocative book *The Children's Machine*, Seymour Papert describes how a first grader named Jennifer, hearing that Papert grew up in Africa, asked him where giraffes put their heads when they sleep.[22] This incident led him to imagine a "Knowledge Machine" where children like Jennifer, who cannot read, can look for videos about any topic in which they are interested, such as the sleeping habits of giraffes. In 1993, when he wrote the book, he thought that such a machine was not more than 2 decades away, and it is technically feasible today. Papert thinks the enormous market potential for such a machine makes it inevitable. In his vision, kids could navigate through it by "speech, touch, or gestures." A kid might ask to see a giraffe sleeping and the system, like Google, would search the vast store of video accumulated in recent years to find such a scene. Papert thinks this would give kids a very powerful toolkit for learning. It would pull the great store of video collected in recent years into a coherent framework.

But, of course, such a machine would not be just for kids. Adults would love online access to the world's store of video material. They could watch an old movie, a Shakespeare play, a star exploding, or a videoconference they wanted to see. If a friend recommends a program that aired recently on TV, they might call it up on demand. In the digital age, libraries are not just for books anymore; they will give people access to all the television programs, movies, video events, and interactive games and simulations that the world has produced.

COMPUTER-BASED LEARNING SOFTWARE

The advent of home computers has led to a proliferation of learning software, some on CD-ROMs and some on the web. The most famous of these are the Sim series, developed by Maxis: *SimCity, The Sims, SimLife, SimEarth, SimAnt,* and so on. In *SimCity,* you are put in charge of developing and running a city, as a kind of dictator. Depending on your decisions, the city and its people may thrive or deteriorate. People who spend time playing the game are learning some of the tradeoffs involved in the dynamics of a city, albeit only those that the game designers have thought to include. *SimLife* similarly teaches about the ecology of systems, *SimEarth* about the dynamics of geology, and *SimAnt* about the behavior of an ant colony. *The Sims* allows people to design a human character to represent them and see how the character's actions play out in a simulated world. It is one of the most popular games now on the market. The Sim series consists of engaging games that teach a variety of subjects, but how much children learn from playing such games depends on how much they think about what they are doing and reflect on the overall ideas and issues that the simulations embody. These games do not, in their current versions, encourage such reflection.

An understanding of video games as learning environments is becoming increasingly important as gaming culture rivals schooling for the attention of children and adolescents across the world. James Paul Gee argues that the compelling nature of video game participation is in part due to the underlying social, cognitive, and developmental learning principles around which successful games are built.[23] With this perspective, games and gaming can be a source for inspiration in building more effective learning environments.

Given this popularity and the compelling nature of game-play, program designers should be able to draw on games and the principles of game design to build more compelling learning environments. In the best-selling game *Civilization,* for example, players have the opportunity to relive the development of global social and economic history. Players must plan, choose to negotiate or fight, acquire and allocate resources, and make decisions to advance their civilization. Taken together, these activities point toward how students can integrate theories and practices from across the curriculum in playing a compelling historical simulation. Of course, the view of history that the game provides is quite different from that found in historical texts, so it may not help students acquire the historical understanding they need for school. Kurt Squire notes how games like *Civilization* can provide opportunities for students who are traditionally not engaged in learning history to "replay" history.[24] Students can investigate, for example, what would have happened if Africans, rather than Europeans, colonized the Americas, and can begin to understand what theories of social change look like in action, rather than in books.

However, there seems to be little constructive information flow across the cultures of school and gaming. The individualistic, immersive nature of play for games, such as *Civilization*, *The Sims*, or *StarWars: Galaxies*, runs counter to the group level, disciplinary, and short duration lessons in most schools. Squire argues that *Civilization* often puts off students and teachers because of the steep learning curve, significant time commitment, and frequent failure experienced by beginners.

In addition to the problems inherent is acquiring gaming literacy, there is a negative reaction to video games and gaming culture among many educators. Video games are regarded as diversionary threats to the integrity of school (at best) or as destructive, compelling activities that simultaneously corrupt moral capacity and create a sedentary, motivation-destroying lifestyle. Apart from embracing a few games such as *Oregon Trail* or *SimCity*, schools have typically acted to control or eliminate gaming. In effect, the content and the addictive play of games such as *Doom*, *Grand Theft Auto*, and *World of Warcraft* have distracted parent groups and school leaders from the compelling nature of game design principles that draws an increasingly broad range of players to gaming.

Gaming culture and game designers seem satisfied to happily exploit this institutional disdain. Games provide increasingly complex, customizable learning-by-doing environments. Just as schools are moving toward increasingly standardizing the learning experience, games offer the prospect of user-defined worlds in which players try out (and get feedback on) their own assumptions, strategies, and identities. Thus, games have come to typify the essentially subversive nature of computing in relation to schools.

Playing video games calls to mind images of solitary players slogging away alone with their computers. The recent teaming of video games with the Internet, however, has opened up new social dimensions for online gaming. Early developments with MUVEs (Multi-User Virtual Environments) allowed people from all over the world to converse by typing or exploring places that others have created for them. Some of these MUVEs, such as *Moose Crossing*, designed by Amy Bruckman, have been created particularly for children.[25] In *Moose Crossing*, children are creating a virtual world out of words, making magical places and creatures that have behaviors. In the process, they are improving their reading and creative writing skills, and learning how to write computer programs.

The next generation of MUVEs consists of graphic-enhanced Massively Multi-Player Online Games (MMOGs) that have led to an explosion of participation in virtual worlds. Edward Castronova analyzed the real-world value of virtual currency used in the MMOG *EverQuest*, based on exchange rates established through online auction sites such as E-bay.com, to document a virtual per-capita gross national product of $2,266—making the *EverQuest* economy the equivalent of the 77th richest country in the world.[26] MMOGs regularly draw millions of players into complex virtual worlds. Although many of these worlds are based on conflict and warfare, which could foster aggressiveness among youth, many players choose to develop trades and become merchants in games such as *Star Wars: Galaxies*. Students who may have little incentive to learn spelling and grammar for teachers in schools soon realize that the penalty for illiteracy in many online games is that they cannot communicate well with valued partners. In an online world, playing video games can take on new social and psychological dimensions.

In recent years, Nicholas Negroponte, who for years headed the Media Lab at MIT, has been developing an inexpensive computer to bring web access into every village in the Third World. The effort is entitled One Laptop Per Child. He had hoped to sell the computer for $100, but sales have lagged and the current price is near $200. The computers are connected to the web through wireless connections powered by solar panels on a village roof. The electrical power for the computer can be provided by a hand crank or foot pedal. The company has made deals with a number of Third World countries, such as Thailand, to buy a large number of the computers. This kind of effort may eventually bring the vast library of web resources to every little village in the world.

There will be a steady accumulation of learning software for both kids and adults. For a generation that has grown up with sophisticated game simulations, learning with modeling technologies is likely to come more easily. Gaming may help them learn a variety of leadership skills, such as resource allocation, negotiating with friends and adversaries, manipulating situations and environments, actively pursuing their goals, and recovering from failures. As John Seely Brown and Douglas Thomas have suggested, the gamers of today may become the leaders of tomorrow.[27]

TECHNICAL CERTIFICATIONS

Until recently, schools and colleges had a monopoly on the certification business. By granting high school diplomas and college degrees, their role was to guarantee that their students had attained a certain level of expertise. This gave them a hold on students: Either stick it out through school and get your degree or you will be handicapped in trying to get a job. The growing use of the GED over the last 30 years as an alternative to the high school diploma has begun to cut into the high school monopoly on certification. But the GED is granted a lower status by employers, and many programs are coordinated through schools and colleges, so the GED has not significantly undercut the hold of schools on certification.

In recent years, a host of companies, such as Microsoft, Cisco, and Novell, as well as technical societies, have started to muscle in on the certification process by offering exams that certify the mastery of technical skill in computer-related occupations. The Cisco Networking Academy, for example, provides a comprehensive training program for network administration.[28] The Cisco Academy is based on a tight linkage of curriculum, learning-by-doing, and assessment activities that are coordinated in a learning environment that blends web-based and classroom learning. Rather than expecting schools to train students in necessary skills, the Cisco Academy partners with schools for classroom space and access to interested students. It has trained more than 400,000 students in 150 countries with a curriculum translated into nine languages. Certification programs like these have, in turn, led to a number of training programs in commercial colleges and community colleges and on the web to prepare students for the certification exams. These certification programs provide an alternative to technical degree programs for students who may struggle with the academic focus of high school and colleges.

These certification programs over the long run are a threat to the monopoly of schools and colleges. Because the certifications are more specific, they are, in fact, more meaningful to potential employers. They specify exactly what skills a student has acquired in a way that a high school diploma or a college degree cannot do. Furthermore, because the certifications are so specific, it is possible to tailor any educational program directed toward them much more carefully. In fact, the companies and technical societies that are developing the certifications have, in many cases, developed very clear specifications as to what and how courses should be taught to prepare people to take the certification exams.

As we argue further in Chapter 8, we suspect that someday it will occur to people that these certifications are more valuable than high school diplomas, in the sense that they specify more precisely what a person can do in some area of knowledge. When that happens, we expect that the technical certification programs will expand beyond technology to many other areas of endeavor, such as travel agents, plumbing, or automotive repair skills. We can imagine both teens and adults working toward getting a variety of different certifications. Pursuing a set of related certifications might even replace the years that teens spend in high school. Alternative certifications may develop a tighter link between what is taught and what is tested in technical fields, in ways the schools and colleges have never been able to achieve.

INTERNET CAFÉS

When one of us was in Bali a few years ago, the prevalence of Internet cafés in the towns and cities was quite striking. All over the world, Internet cafés are springing up, where people can go and log on to the web for a small fee. These cafés are like the libraries of the future in providing access to all the resources of the web. Their counterparts in America are coffeeshops and other venues where people gather to access the web. They particularly attract young people, who spend hours engaging in conversations and games, reading about what is happening in the world, learning how to program, or exploring different sites that relate to their interests.

Some countries, such as China, have tried to restrict access to the web in order to prevent people from learning about things that the government does not approve of. Despite such efforts, Internet cafés have sprung up all over China, and some people will always find ways around the barriers that governments put in place to block access to different sites. The explosion of Internet cafés has made efforts to control access to web sites a hopeless task for many national governments.

More and more of the world's accumulated knowledge is spreading to the web. Hence, with access to the web in many locations, people can begin to educate themselves. This is the role that public libraries have played in the past. As people all over the world see that an education is necessary to prosper in a technological society, they are likely to start teaching themselves through the resources of the web. Of course, it will be difficult for most people to find the information they want unless they develop web search and evaluation skills, but a culture may develop among Internet café goers for helping people carry out searches or strategize in playing games.

Cafés are also opening new venues for online social interaction, which often can seem ominous. In South Korea, the online games *Lineage* and *Lineage II* involve hundreds of thousands of players in a medieval warfare world pitting dozens of clan-based player alliances against one another. *Lineage* is often played nonstop in cafés, called "PC bangs," that provide a site for participation in virtual worlds. Sometimes the lines between the worlds blur, as in 2001, when members of one online clan whose leader had been killed in the game savagely attacked the real-world player responsible.[29] Inexpensive access to the web through cafés provides the whole world with access to knowledge, new social arrangements, and new ways of thinking about learning. Of course, Internet cafés also provide a venue for kids to waste an enormous amount of time.

LIFELONG LEARNING

When taken together, the cumulative effect of these innovations is to extend learning throughout life and over many venues. With time, these pieces might come to comprise the fragments of a new system of education in which schools are pushed to the peripheral role in learning that they once occupied in the era of apprenticeship. But for now, these elements have developed independently of one another. They do not in any sense form a coherent system of education. That is where the need for visionaries is most apparent. It will take a new group of energetic visionaries to once again do the kind of work that Horace Mann and his colleagues did— that is, to figure out how to build an equitable and coherent system from these emergent technological pieces.

Some aspects of the present school system are likely to endure. Elementary schools, for example, which provide childcare and early socialization processes, are likely to remain as they have been. They may, however, have to adapt to an influx of inexpensive laptop computers. Elementary schools have always been the cornerstone of the K–12 system, and young children will always need guidance and instruction in reading, writing, and arithmetic.

But video games and learning centers are already putting up a challenge for the attention of middle school students, and with technical certification, distance education, and adult education providing options for high school students who are disengaged from the present system, the fragments of the new system are already signaling how high schools may become anachronisms. The remaining chapters will consider where these changes may be taking us.

These technological developments raise concerns about equity, social behavior, and the cultural cohesion of society. In the remaining chapters, we argue that it is important for society to begin thinking more broadly about how to deal with these new developments in order to address the issues and problems they raise for teaching and learning. Limiting our concerns about learning with new technologies to schools can blind us to important issues and possibilities. We challenge readers to think beyond schools, to consider how technology can be brought to bear to address issues of equity and the implications of these developments for education in the future.

6

The Three Eras
of Education

We are now entering the lifelong-learning era of education, having experienced the apprenticeship and universal-schooling eras. These three eras differ in many aspects, but in some ways the lifelong-learning era seems to reflect elements of the earlier apprenticeship era.

As we moved from the apprenticeship era to the universal-schooling era, there were changes on a number of different dimensions: Who was responsible for children's education, what was the purpose and the content of their education, how were they to be taught and assessed, and what did we expect them to learn. There were also changes in the location of where learning occurred, the culture in which learning occurred, and the relationships between teachers and learners. All these aspects of education are changing once again as we move into the era of lifelong learning.

RESPONSIBILITY: FROM PARENTS TO THE STATE
TO INDIVIDUALS AND PARENTS

Perhaps the most revolutionary idea advanced by Horace Mann and his colleagues was for the state to take over responsibility for educating children from their parents. In the apprenticeship era, parents decided what their children would learn. Parents would often decide what occupation a boy would pursue, and either the father would train him if he was to follow in the father's footsteps, or the boy would be apprenticed to a relative or friend to learn a trade. Girls learned their household and other duties from their mothers. If they lived on a farm, as was most common, mothers would teach the girls their farm duties, such as milking cows. If the family was in a trade, the mother would often run the shop and the girls would learn how to do that. If the mother was a midwife, the girls would learn midwifery by observing their mother and slowly taking on some of her responsibilities. Many of the learned people in the apprenticeship era were largely self-taught, as the story of Abraham Lincoln reading at night by the fire illustrates.

With the onset of the Industrial Revolution, there was a concern about immigrant children learning the values and language of America, and a sense that this would be the responsibility of the state, not of parents. The reformers felt that immigrant parents could not teach their children proper American values. And so Horace Mann and his colleagues argued that we needed to require all children to go to school, where they would learn American values and the English language. The mass education model of industrial-age schools allowed for large groups of children to receive instruction in a common curriculum. Mann felt that participation in a common base of knowledge, language, and social interaction would make it possible for all children to grow up to be successful American citizens. So the reformers advocated taking control of education from the parents and giving it to the state. This often led to children developing attitudes and values that their parents did not share. A graphic description of this process is beautifully described in Richard Rodriguez's autobiographical book, *Hunger of Memory*, where he describes how he was torn between his parents' values and the American values he acquired from his schooling.[1] Now the home-schooling movement is trying to take responsibility for children's education back from the state.

In the present lifelong-learning era, responsibility for education is shifting away from the state and back to the parents (for younger children) and to the individual (for teenagers and adults). This movement reflects the emphasis on customizing education to the particular learners' needs, interests, and abilities. We see this in the growth of home schooling, distance education, and learning centers. More and more parents are taking control of the education of their children by buying them educational videos and computer software, by teaching them what they think is important, and by purchasing educational services for them when they face difficulties or show interest in a particular topic. When people get older, starting sometime in their teens, they are deciding what they want to learn, either out of a desire to advance their careers or to pursue their deep interests. Many of the technology stories we hear are of teens pursuing individual goals, such as making web pages or remixing music videos. Bill Gates is famous for spending hours in his high school years programming computers. Although high schools offer some choices, technology makes it easier for teens to pursue their individual passions on their own.

EXPECTATIONS: FROM SOCIAL REPRODUCTION TO SUCCESS FOR ALL TO INDIVIDUAL CHOICE

Before the Industrial Revolution, parents wanted their children to follow in their footsteps. And so the education they expected for their children was the same education they had acquired. If they were farmers, the children were expected to learn to be farmers like their parents. If they were engaged in trade or a craft, their children were expected to learn to carry on that trade or craft. If they read the Bible, children were expected to learn to read just as they did. These expectations supported reproduction of class differences. There was little room for social mobility that would allow children to advance themselves by getting a good education. There was an assumption of social stability and that children would face a world much like the one their parents had faced. So the goal was to raise children with the same skills their parents had.

After the Industrial Revolution, one of the main arguments that Horace Mann made was that education could bring everyone up to a common, high level of success. He wanted to make it possible for the children of immigrants from different countries to achieve the American dream. Much of the American dream consisted of the promise that hard work and a good education would pay off in rising social and economic status, and that American society had the kind of social mobility that would allow everyone to advance. Creating a common school system would be the central path for children to take advantage of social mobility. The flip side of imposing school on everyone was to socialize children away from their parents' goals and values, in order to foster social cohesion and common civic values. Mann felt that if children were provided a free education, they would adopt American values and have the skills needed to do any kind of work they chose. This is an argument for equity through education, which comes down to us in the phrase "Every child can learn." Eventually, many parents bought into this ideology, and came to expect their children to acquire a good education. In fact, it became a dream of many parents that their children would attend one of the elite colleges in America, even though they themselves may never have finished high school or gone to college. But there is still a feeling among many families, especially immigrants from other countries, that the schools are educating their children with a set of values that are inimical to their own.

We think that the expectations for education are beginning to change once again. The goal of success for all is still widely present. But teenagers and young adults are taking on more responsibility for their own lives and education. They often reject what school has to offer, choosing to pursue instead whatever interests them or what they think is necessary to advance their careers. They are less willing to accept the expectations of educators, who, following in Mann's footsteps, have decreed what an educated person should know through their curriculum standards. Rather, in the spirit of customization, many young people are pursuing their own educational paths, learning what they think will be of value to them. Choice reigns in charter schools, rich curricular electives, and virtual schooling options. Home schooling is the parents' way of saying that we think we should decide what our children should learn. Distance education, learning centers, and technical certifications all act to expand the choices that people can make for what they will learn. In this light, the standards movement can be seen as a conservative check on rampant customization. As the lifelong-learning era moves gradually toward a situation where people choose for themselves what kind of education they will obtain, standards will serve as a constraint on the range of what counts as legitimate learning.

CONTENT: FROM PRACTICAL SKILLS TO DISCIPLINARY KNOWLEDGE TO LEARNING HOW TO LEARN

Before the Industrial Revolution, the major purposes of educating children were for religious salvation and to help them learn to do the work that they would perform as adults. The content of education focused on literacy and on the skills and crafts of their parents or their masters, if they were apprenticed to someone other than their parents. The schools at the time taught a few basic skills, such as reading, writing, and basic computation, which children would need to read the Bible and carry out tasks such as buying and selling goods. But few students went to school for more than a year or 2, so the content of their school education was fairly basic. They did, however, learn a lot from helping their parents at work and doing chores around the house. Most children learned how to make a living from their parents, but when a child was apprenticed in a craft or trade, the master took on the role of a parent to ensure that the child learned the skills he or she would need to succeed. Hence, the major portion of a child's education focused on the practical skills of making a living.

With the Industrial Revolution, the important goals of education became social cohesion and preparing children to live in a democratic society. Mass public schooling began to separate the religious and vocational content of education. The schools stressed learning a common core of secular knowledge—particularly reading, writing, and arithmetic—which children would need to function as intelligent citizens and workers. As schooling was extended through high school, the curriculum added knowledge in the different disciplines that had developed in the modern era. History, English, and civics were stressed to prepare students to be good citizens. Courses in algebra and geometry were added in order to prepare students for the many professions that required mathematical training, such as the financial, engineering, and scientific professions. The Committee of Ten, which the U.S. commissioner of education convened in the 1890s, decided that every high school student should take a set of courses—English, mathematics, Latin and Greek, history, science, and geography—that reflected the disciplines that colleges felt were important. The committee's recommendations largely determined the high school curriculum in the 20th century, though Latin and Greek did drop out in favor of modern foreign languages. However, except in parochial schools, religious education was left unaddressed by secular public schooling and continued mainly through family-based, apprenticeship models.

With the knowledge explosion, it is becoming impossible for schools to teach people all the knowledge they might need as adults. Extending schooling for more and more years to accommodate the explosion of new knowledge and the growing demands for education is not a viable strategy. So learning how to learn and learning how to find useful resources are becoming the most important goals of education. Therefore, the focus is more on generic skills, such as problem solving and communication in different media, on interpersonal skills in order to interact with people from different backgrounds, and on learning to find information and resources and to learn from them. These ideas were outlined in a report from the U.S. Labor Department in 1991 called the SCANS report.[2] It argued that in order to be prepared for work in the 21st century, people needed education in five areas, called core competencies:

- Resources: Identifying, organizing, planning, and allocating resources
- Interpersonal: Working with others

- Information: Acquiring and using information
- Systems: Understanding complex interrelationships
- Technology: Working with a variety of technologies

The SCANS report argued that these new competencies should be built upon a foundation of basic skills, thinking skills, and interpersonal qualities, such as responsibility and integrity. The SCANS report is a symptom of the changing demands on education. Over the last century, routine jobs have been disappearing, and the demand for flexibility and thinking has grown. People will have to keep learning new knowledge and skills throughout their lifetimes, as their lives and jobs keep changing.

Another implication of the individualization that results when institutions can no longer control access to content is that it becomes increasingly difficult to separate religious and secular values. When learners select programs of study based on their interests, then the values that guide learner interests become integrated into the education experience. A cursory look at blogs and social network sites demonstrates how not only religious but other shared values rooted in popular culture, sports, and entertainment permeate new technology learning environments. This suggests that the explosion of learning content out of the control of constraining institutions allows learners to customize learning experiences in terms of personal, rather than institutional, values and beliefs.

PEDAGOGY: FROM APPRENTICESHIP
TO DIDACTICISM TO INTERACTION

The pedagogy of apprenticeship involves modeling, observation, coaching, and practice. The adult shows how to do things and then watches while the learner tries, providing less support as the learner gains experience. Apprenticeship was not simply the method of teaching trades and crafts. It was how children learned how to run a farm or shop, how to be a midwife, how to do chores around the house, and even how to read and write when these skills were taught at home. It is the natural way that people teach other people in a one-on-one situation. Apprenticeship is very resource intensive, since it requires a knowledgeable adult for every two or three learners. However, it is very efficient because almost everyone manages to learn, given such close supervision. In the family, older siblings might take on some of the burden of teaching, and in the trades, a master might have a number of apprentices at different levels of expertise, who help teach novices.

Apprenticeship was not a viable pedagogy for mass schooling. When the schools were flooded with students, they had to evolve a mass pedagogy that would work for a very high ratio of students to teachers. The pedagogy of industrial-era schooling involved small numbers of teachers lecturing to large numbers of children about knowledge and skills, directing the children to practice by answering questions or doing homework, then testing to see if they had learned what was taught. Lecturing proved to be the simplest pedagogy to implement, since teachers need no resources other than their knowledge, which they try to communicate to students. The progressive educators argued that children learn better by active engagement rather than listening to teachers, and so new methods that engaged students were adopted over time. These included having children answer questions, recite things they had learned, fill out worksheets, do homework, and engage in projects and discussions. The pedagogy of schooling has evolved a long way from the early years, when, as Larry Cuban describes, students were expected to recite in order the names of all the bays along the east coast of America.[3] But it is still a mass-production pedagogy, where many students fail to learn what is taught.

The pedagogy of the lifelong-learning era is evolving toward reliance on interaction. Sometimes this involves interacting with a rich technological environment such as a computer tutor or a game on the web and sometimes with other people by means of a computer network. The pedagogy of computer tutors echoes the apprenticeship model in setting individualized tasks for learners and offering guidance and feedback as they work. Computer tutors provide a variety of computer tools that support learners in carrying out tasks. For example, students might be given the task of solving a complex geometry problem, such as finding the area within a circle but outside an inscribed right triangle. If the student does not know how to start, the system might provide a hint, such as asking if the student knows how to find the area of a right triangle. If the student needs more help, further hints might be provided, such as showing the right triangle as half of a rectangle, and asking whether the student knows how to find the area of the rectangle. As the student works through the problem, the system could track any errors the student makes and provide feedback ("Are you sure that is correct?"). When the student completes the problem, the computer might review the procedure with the student, pointing out the critical steps to solve the problem and the general ideas that the problem encompasses.

This type of guided pedagogy extends beyond the world of computer tutors. For example, discussion-board interest groups can provide specific, task-level advice about how to solve a video game puzzle, whether to make a fantasy baseball trade, or how much automobile stock should be purchased to balance a portfolio. As another example, a distance-learning teacher might closely monitor how a group of students is progressing on a project they have been assigned. Computers can extend the kind of close, personal supervision provided in apprenticeship methods to every learner, either by monitoring actions the learner takes in a computer environment or by providing a trace of student work to a distant teacher. But the downside is that learners working in such environments may become more isolated from social interaction with other people.

ASSESSMENT: FROM OBSERVATION TO TESTING TO EMBEDDED ASSESSMENT

In the apprenticeship era, the adult carefully observed learners and corrected them as they went along, giving them tasks they were ready for, and seeing whether they completed them successfully. Observation during the course of task completion combined the functions of formative and summative assessment. Ongoing, formative encouragement or critique provided feedback to guide the learner through tasks, and the final, summative judgment gave learners feedback on whether the task was successfully completed. Such close supervision keeps learners from making a lot of mistakes, since the adult comes to understand the capabilities of learners, and can anticipate many of the problems they may have. The master can ward off failure by giving tasks that have the right amount of challenge— not so easy that learners become bored and not so difficult that they fail. When learners do make mistakes, the master can go over what was done and try to identify what led to any mistake. Assessment in this context, then, does not involve getting a grade or failing a test. It simply means getting feedback as you work, and suggestions as to how to improve. The master comes away with a clear understanding of what each apprentice is capable of doing; the student comes away with an assessment of just what still needs to be learned.

In the schooling era, standardized testing emerged as the means to determine whether students had acquired the skills and knowledge that had been taught. Standardized testing effectively separated formative and summative assessment. As with apprenticeship, the teacher's role was to formatively observe the student to provide direct feedback on the progress of learning. But teachers often could not assess the cumulative effects of the curriculum over time, so tests were developed to track whether students had learned enough to advance to the next level. In order to make sure that all students in a classroom were at about the same level, tests were also used to place students in a particular class and to determine whether they had learned the material well enough before passing learners on to the next grade. Testing always involves some cutoff, so testing brought with it the notions of passing and failing. This led to the ranking of students, and ultimately, to a sense of failure among those who do not learn as easily as others do.

In the lifelong-learning era, as with apprenticeship, summative and formative assessment begin to converge. This is particularly true in computer-based learning environments. Here, assessment occurs as the learner progresses through the tasks in order to provide ongoing support to determine whether the learner has accomplished the goals. This kind of assessment is more like that in apprenticeship settings, where the assessment is ongoing and tightly coupled to the learning. When students need help, the computer may provide hints or suggestions as to how to proceed. When students make a mistake, the computer might point out the error or guide them toward the correct answer. By embedding assessment into the ongoing learning process, it takes much of the onus off making mistakes. To the degree that the computer can provide the appropriate support, it can ensure that everyone succeeds and feels a sense of accomplishment.

LOCATION: FROM HOME TO SCHOOL TO ANYWHERE

In the apprenticeship era, most work was comprised of household and domestic industries. Children learned to carry out adult tasks from parents or relatives at home. In towns and cities, children might be sent to school for a year or 2, but that is not where most learning occurred. The main venue for education was the home, and the farm or shop attached to it.

With the Industrial Revolution, parents started working outside the home, and so children were gathered in schools to learn things they would need in later life. Gradually, school came to be seen as the major venue where education happens. Even workplaces, such as in the military and business, created school-like settings when they wanted to train people to do some task. Norman Frederiksen told the story of how he was assigned to improve the assessment of gunner's mates for the navy during World War II.[4] This is a job that requires cleaning and maintaining guns onboard ships, but he found that the teaching was by lecture and the testing was by paper and pencil. He proposed to institute a performance test, based on the tasks that gunner's mates actually carry out. The instructors objected to this, because they thought the students would fail. Just as the instructors predicted, the learners all failed the performance test, but Frederiksen insisted that the new test be kept. After they failed, students demanded to be taught how to do the tasks on which they would be tested. Soon they learned to do just as well on the performance test as they had previously done on the pencil-and-paper test. This story illustrates that when we view education through the lens of school, we try to make education fit into the school mold, even if it doesn't make a lot of sense to do so. And that is what most education in the military and business still looks like.

Now education is moving into many different venues, where learning materials can be accessed from computers and the web. Lifelong learners often use tools such as personal digital assistants that they carry with them, which can be connected to the Internet, to access their learning environments and communities. Many towns and buildings are providing wireless connections, and this connectivity is spreading rapidly. We are approaching the era when people can engage in just-in-time learning anytime and anywhere.

CULTURE: FROM ADULT CULTURE TO PEER CULTURE TO MIXED-AGE CULTURE

Before the Industrial Revolution, children learned in the context of the adults who were working around them. The work they were doing was essential, and the children were treated as helpers rather than students. Hence, the children felt the importance of what they were learning and that they were an integral part of the work group. While they might form close bonds with their brothers and sisters, or fellow apprentices, no strong peer culture arose in that setting. The work was serious business, and their learning to do the work was crucial to their own and their family's survival. The notion that there was a separate youth culture, or even adolescence as a developmental category, did not emerge in the apprenticeship era. Children were regarded as small adults, and what youth culture there was largely reflected the activities and experiences that adults thought would be appropriate for youth.

As James Coleman points out, a separate youth peer culture arose with the advent of industrial-age schooling.[5] This new peer culture reflected the opinions of adolescents and, as the 20th century progressed, often ran counter to the expectations and values of adult culture. Middle schools and high schools concentrated same-age children together, which led to the development of peer culture. Kids have to be old enough and concentrated enough to form a community that has its own beliefs and values. When peer culture did develop, it began to reflect the newly recognized needs of an adolescent class. Often, peer culture emphasized the difference between the cultures of schooling and youth.

Penelope Eckert described how peer culture in a typical American high school had developed between two poles: the jock culture and the burnout culture. [6] The jock culture consisted of all the students who fully participated in school activities and played the school game. The burnouts were the students who were hostile to the school and teachers, often doing drugs or other nonschool activities. While Eckert found that most students fell in between these two groups, the two formed the axis around which the school culture revolved. Economic expansion in mid-century America reinforced the development of adolescent peer culture as marketers discovered disposable teen income. This peer culture transformed the entertainment, fashion, and advertising industries, and became a distracting contender for the attention of youth who did not find a home in the culture of schools.

As learning moves out of a school setting, peer culture may weaken when children are working on tasks with their parents and other adults, or in a media environment. Home schooling is a movement designed to remove children from peer culture. Many parents do not like the values their children get from their peers, and they think that by schooling kids at home, they can protect them from the influences of peers, and from the wider society in general. To the degree that learning centers take hold as an institution, they too may undercut youth culture. In the community technology centers, people of different ages come to learn and use the facilities. So there is a mixed-age population all learning and working together, which acts to subdue the effects of peers. And when students are learning from distance education, they will be rather isolated from others, except to the degree that they are doing online projects with other people. It would be very difficult for peer culture to develop among online participants in distance education, since the learners only interact in order to accomplish a specific task or discuss a specific issue. In general, as education becomes a lifelong activity, there are likely to be more situations where adults and children are learning together. This will tend to create a new kind of mixed-age learning culture.

RELATIONSHIPS: FROM PERSONAL BONDS TO AUTHORITY FIGURES TO COMPUTER-MEDIATED INTERACTION

In the apprenticeship era, children were learning from the adults they grew up with and knew very well. Most of children's education came from their parents or close relatives and friends. These were people who were concerned for their future. So children formed close bonds with the people who were teaching them. The closeness of the bonds had many salutary effects on their learning. Children knew that if they did not try hard, they would disappoint people who were critical to their survival. In times of poverty and limited opportunity, a child's failure to learn in apprenticeship had real consequences for families. So most children made a real effort to be responsible, and to learn as much as they could in order to please the adults who were teaching them. And because the adults knew the children well, they could tailor their teaching to the children's needs, interests, and abilities. In fact, much the same thing happens today among parents who school their children at home.

With the advent of universal schooling, children and their teachers only meet one another on the first day of class. They are strangers at the outset. Though many teachers develop bonds with their students, they do not have the time parents have to develop a deep understanding of their students' personal needs and abilities. Many-to-one student-teacher ratios make it difficult to build the same kinds of relationships seen in apprenticeship. The ability to establish enduring learning relationships with students usually depends on whether the teacher demonstrates the authority to control the classroom. In most middle and high schools, teachers have to establish their authority from the outset or they will not survive very long. It is the students who perceive the value of schooling to their futures who are most likely to pay the respect to teachers that is necessary to make schooling work. There is a clear cultural component to the giving and receiving of authority in schools.

As Lisa Delpit suggests, many teachers belong to a white middle-class culture that expects authority to be given to one who achieves an authoritative role. On the other hand, Delpit suggests that many people of color "expect authority to be earned by personal effort and exhibited by personal characteristics."[7] These contrasting perceptions of given versus earned authority have contributed to a two-tier model of mass schooling, one for students who are freely willing to respect the role of the teacher and the other for students who expect teachers to earn their authority. The kinds of learning environments that develop in the first tier, where authority issues do not come into play, are significantly different from environments where the teacher's authority is always in question. Researchers such as Ron Ferguson emphasize that restoring these teacher-student relationships is an important factor in improving learning for students who traditionally struggle in schools.[8]

Lifelong learning restores some of the relationship characteristics of apprenticeship learning. Interest-based learning thrives when participants develop multiple connections across learning communities. Many of these relationships reflect the kinds of mentor-student interactions that are characteristic of apprenticeship learning. When students take distance education courses, they interact with teachers and other students over the Internet based on common interests. Online relationships allow teachers to focus much more on feedback concerning learning process and outcomes. Afterschool learning environments are also built on restoring the kinds of personal interaction that have been lost for students who feel they don't belong in schools.

Computer-based learning environments impact the learning relationship in another way. Computer systems have limited understanding of students as individuals and do not provide the warmth and support of a good human teacher. At the same time, the systems provide regular, targeted feedback in a noncritical, impartial manner. Much is lost in computer-based learning settings, since we learn most naturally by interacting with people we know well and respect. But the highly interactive nature of computer environments may, in part, compensate for the lack of personal bonds. Given the limitations of computer environments, it will be best if students working in computer-mediated environments are part of a community, either offline with friends and family, or online with people who share common interests.

CRITICAL TRANSFORMATIONS IN EDUCATION

Perhaps the most striking change from the era of apprenticeship to the era of universal schooling was the state's assumption of responsibility for educating children. The state control of education led to a mass-schooling model that aggregated students in age groups, promoted standardized curriculum and assessments, and reconfigured the relationship between teachers and learners. We think that in the lifelong-learning era, people interested in advancing their own learning will begin to take back responsibility for education from the state. But at the same time, what will happen to learners who are unwilling or unable to take advantage of the technologies that drive the diverse lifelong-learning environment?

7

What May Be Lost and
What May Be Gained

The revolution in education will alter not just the lives of students, but all of our modern society. As with any revolution, there will be both gains and losses. Some pessimists see people becoming subservient to their technologies and many people being left behind as technology comes to dominate our lives. Some optimists see a golden age of learning opening before us, in which people will be able to find resources to pursue any education they may want. What lies before us? We don't envision a future that is either bleak or idyllic, but one with elements of both. In this chapter, we consider the worst fears and the most optimistic hopes. By facing the range of possible outcomes, society can make wiser choices to mitigate the dangers and foster the possibilities.

WHAT MAY BE LOST

In Thomas Jefferson's and Horace Mann's vision, education would prepare people to be good citizens and assimilate them into a common culture. Mann was very concerned about educating immigrants and developing social cohesion. Much of this cohesion may be lost as parents and individuals take over responsibility for learning and there is fracturing of education into smaller groups. We can anticipate not only Christian conservatives developing curricula, as they are already doing in home and private schooling, but many different interest groups, such as environmentalists, Muslims, Mormons, Cuban Americans, Mexican Americans, and so forth, developing curricula that address the concerns they have about raising children. As David Brooks argues, we are settling into our own little "cultural zones" where like-minded people cluster together.[1]

Through such fracturing into interest groups, citizenship and social co-hesion goals are likely to be undermined. When the American republic was new, there was a general concern with whether it could hold together as a single union, given how diverse the people and their values were in the dif-ferent states. These differences came to a head in the Civil War. By the 20th century, however, the fear of the Union breaking apart had diminished con-siderably. In fact, modern media, such as television, have had a very strong homogenizing effect on the population, which ensures a common culture without depending on schools to produce one. But that effect may be lost as media outlets proliferate with streaming media and multiple channels.

We see diversity expanding in the movements toward multiculturalism and the mainstreaming of minority groups, such as the handicapped. Of course, there has been a significant backlash against multiculturalism, as evidenced by English-only laws and the movement against bilingual edu-cation. But the fear of society breaking apart is not nearly as great as it once was, and so the demand that public schools must help Americanize the di-verse peoples in America has lost some of its force. Hence, we are willing to let different groups go their separate ways in private schools and home schooling. In fact, the push for vouchers and charter schools is an effort to let parents take control of their children's education from the state. These trends can only lead to more diversity among Americans, despite the countervailing force of the mass media.

One of the most serious issues that a diminution of the role of public school portends is the problem of equity of access to learning. We see this concern in the discussion of the "digital divide": i.e., the difference in ac-cess to computers and the web between rich and poor, and white and non-white people. Schools have been the means by which many immigrants and minorities gained access to the American mainstream. Even today, despite widespread tracking and segregation, the public schools are the institution that fosters equity more than any other institution in America. As Martin Carnoy and Henry Levin argue, "Schooling produces relatively more equal outcomes than the workplace and other institutions of the larger society."[2] If different groups take over the education of their children, then many poor and minority children are likely to suffer. The danger is that public schools may be left with uninterested students, while parents who want to give their children a good education avail themselves of home schooling, private schools, and learning centers.

In recent years, education has been perceived by parents as more and more critical to "getting ahead" in America. This reflects the growing disparity in income between college-educated and non-college-educated people.[3] Even though schools have instituted policies to help some students get ahead, such as gifted and talented programs, Advanced Placement courses, and tracking, public schools were conceived to be egalitarian institutions. Hence, parents are spending more money in recent years to buy their children educational services, such as educational videos and games, computer-based resources, private schooling, and specialized tutoring, so that their children will have an advantage. Poor and less educated people cannot buy these services, and may not even be aware that they exist, which will exacerbate the educational inequalities that the public schools have tried to mitigate.

There is also the potential decline of liberal arts as education becomes more centered on the individual. Will people seek out the kind of education that broadens them as people? When people select their own education goals, they tend to select things that interest them or that are occupation-oriented. Their choices are often narrowly focused. A major goal of education has been to extend students' horizons. In the future, will children be steered along narrow paths that their parents approve of, such as a particular religious or job orientation? This may make it difficult for people to get along with people who come from different backgrounds or have different views. Further, children may be very limited in the occupations they consider, because parents may try to limit their children's choices, as their choices used to be limited in societies before the spread of schooling. It is clear that public schooling has produced a much more tolerant society, where people encounter many different ideas and types of people. Will this all be cut short by the Balkanization of education?

Finally, will people become more isolated, sitting at home in front of a computer and interacting less with other people socially? It is by interacting with supportive mentors and teachers that people are inspired to work hard and learn difficult topics. Isolation could produce a loss of social skills and societal cohesion. There was a study carried out at Carnegie-Mellon University on home computer users who had just started using the Internet.[4] The research found that spending time on the Internet was associated with decreases in talking among family members, reductions in the number of friends and acquaintances they kept up with, and increases in depression and loneliness. This was true even though people in the study heavily used email and other communication services on the Internet. One danger, then, of increased use of computers for education is that many people will isolate themselves more from friends and family. The decline in the number of people participating in community organizations has already been well documented by Robert Putnam.[5] We worry that the technologizing of education will further the decline in community among Americans, at the same time that the population is becoming more diverse.

Many of these problems are exacerbated by the privatization trend that took hold during the 1980s. There has been an increasing inclination worldwide, but particularly in the United States, to encourage people to fend for themselves. Although this allows savvy people to make more of their own choices and purchase their own educational resources, it leaves less educated or affluent people further behind in the competition for educational resources. In Ontario, Canada, about 24% of parents with school-age children have hired tutors, and 50% claim that they would hire tutors if they could afford them.[6] Similar percentages are found in the United States. Privatization has the effect of increasing educational disparities among the population between the rich and the poor. Technology so far has been a force for increasing inequality rather than decreasing inequality.

To summarize the pessimistic view of the future, we see the current equity issues in education increasing with the penetration of technology into education. More and more now, the commercialization of education means that the elites are buying resources in order to give their children an edge in the education race. They buy lots of educational toys and videos for their children when they are preschoolers. They send them to expensive preschools. They buy them computers at an early age, so they can learn to navigate the web and acquire critical technology skills. They send them to private schools or buy houses in neighborhoods with elite public schools. They contribute time and resources to their children's schools, so they will be able to provide the kids with the best possible schooling. They get their kids tutoring if they are having trouble with any of their classes. They send them to SAT and ACT prep courses at local learning centers. In short, they are buying their kids the best possible education so they can beat the competition in later life.

State courts have tried to restore equity by mandating that states distribute resources more fairly among their towns and cities. But many elites resist such redistribution of resources with all their might. One rich county in Vermont, when faced with a mandate to redistribute finances to poorer counties in the state, actually tried to secede from Vermont and join New Hampshire, across the river. It is going to be very difficult to reallocate resources more fairly among different schools across the country, and the availability now of vast technological resources only exacerbates the problem. To redress the problem will take a much broader vision of education than educators now have.

WHAT MAY BE GAINED

One of the most powerful promises offered by technology is that learning will become more engaging. Education will be directed more toward what people want to learn, and hence, they will be more excited and drawn to learning. For example, parents who are schooling their children at home usually encourage them to pursue topics they are interested in more deeply than other topics. They try to embed important learning goals, such as math and writing, in those contexts, so that the children devote themselves to doing a good job. Furthermore, when people choose courses to take in distance education or adult education, they choose topics that they feel will help their careers or that reflect abiding interests they have. And, of course, when people watch television or purchase educational videos, games, or simulations, they choose topics that interest them. So they are much more likely than schoolchildren to be engaged in their learning.

Despite its effect in increasing inequity, the commercialization of education may act to increase students' engagement in learning. Products developed by commercial firms, whether courses, videos, or software, will be designed to attract buyers. Hence, as has been done at the University of Phoenix, large efforts will be made to produce a product that people will purchase. And the competition will be fierce. The commercial education market is clearly growing rapidly, and many new firms are entering it, such as Sylvan and Kaplan. They are developing new approaches to education that clearly appeal to people. As the monopoly of the district school comes undone, it will free educational institutions and products to compete for students. But the question remains: Who will be buying, and how?

Another potential gain stems from the capability of computers to customize education to the particular needs and abilities of individual learners. Computer learning environments can be designed to provide hints and support to students when they need help. This support can be carefully allocated, so that students get as much help as they need, but not too much. This allows learners to tackle tasks that they might not otherwise be able to attempt, and to succeed when they do. Hence, learners can be given tasks that are challenging to them, where they learn a lot and feel a sense of accomplishment upon completing the tasks. In this way, computer environments can adapt to the level of the student's ability and help all students to succeed.

Technology also can make it possible to access knowledge anytime, anywhere, through the web. Universal access to learning would have profound effects. If people are at home with an Internet connection, in the future, they may have available all the world's knowledge at their fingertips—not just in the form of text, but in videos, tutorials, and simulations. In an ideal world, universal access may even be provided to poor people around the world. The One Laptop per Child effort seeks to make this dream a reality. Whether we will see this happen is an open question, but the possibility is staggering.

As education becomes more tailored to people's interests and abilities, the kind of competition between students found in school will likely diminish. In the apprenticeship era, Jean Lave argues that almost everyone successfully learned the skills they were taught.[7] One of the fundamental problems of school is that children are always comparing themselves to other students, and it is only the best students who feel they are successful. Because school is so competitive, a sense of failure overwhelms many students. Most cope by turning their energies to other activities, such as sports or doing drugs. The majority of students come to regard learning as something to do as little as possible. The goal becomes to get grades that are good enough not to hurt one's future, with a minimum of effort. This pervasive attitude is inimical to learning and is a direct product of the competitive nature of school, where only a few students look smart. In a technology-rich environment, people are more likely to go their own way in learning, so they will not feel the sense of failure that comes when everyone is supposed to be learning the same thing at the same time.

Finally, it is important to note that turning education over to the parents and the individual transfers responsibility for learning onto the family. Parents who school their children at home can provide a level of attention to their learning that simply does not happen consistently in schools. The children feel the pressure to learn and it shows in their performance on standardized tests, as we noted earlier in Chapter 5. But parents also try to instill a sense of responsibility in the children themselves, by giving them tasks to do and expecting them to carry those tasks out.

If people are learning at work or at home using distance education, they are similarly forced to take responsibility for their own learning. When the state took over responsibility for teaching children, families and indi-

viduals ceded most of the responsibility to the schools. Many schoolchildren seem to defy the schools to teach them anything. But people are not
going to learn much unless they take responsibility for their own learning.
Teachers struggle to inspire students to take responsibility for their learning, and many succeed, but many also fail. Technology may help put students more in charge of their own learning.

REALIZING THE PROMISE AND MITIGATING THE DANGERS

Our hope is that as more children and adults become aware of how
critical education is to success, more and more segments of society will avail
themselves of the new opportunities that these technology-based resources
make possible. We also hope that as technology becomes cheaper and more
technology-based resources become available, most people will be able to
afford to purchase the educational resources they desire. But these are mere
hopes, and it is not at all clear that they will be realized.

Whether the potential losses outweigh the potential gains of the emerging education system remains a matter for debate. How society acts to take
advantage of the promise and mitigate the dangers is an issue of immediate concern. Technology holds the promise for engaging students in deep
learning and pushing students to become the best-educated people they
can be. We as a society should think about how to make that promise come
to fruition. How can the schools tap into the technology revolution most
effectively? And how can we capitalize on the technology resources outside of the schools?

8

How Schools Can Cope with the New Technologies

To effectively incorporate technology into schools, educators must understand the imperatives of the technologies that are driving this revolution. We have encapsulated those imperatives as *customization, interaction*, and *learner control. Customization* refers to providing people with the knowledge they want when they want it and supporting and guiding people individually as they learn. *Interaction* refers to the ability of computers to give learners immediate feedback and to engage learners actively in accomplishing realistic tasks. *Learner control* refers to putting learners in charge of their own learning whenever possible, so that they feel ownership and can direct their learning wherever their interests take them.

We face the current challenges of schooling at a time when the pendulum of education policy is swinging away from local control toward standards and accountability. In an effort to provide equality of outcomes, federal and state policies have emphasized accountability by promoting standardized educational outcomes and pressuring schools to adopt uniform practices in classrooms. Particularly in urban areas, this emphasis on accountability is providing mixed results. The new accountability policies have made some headway in improving student achievement across the country as measured by standardized tests.[1] Still, high-stakes testing runs the risk of encouraging educators to "game" the system, producing reportable results without real improvements to student learning.[2] And the new policies that pressure schools to provide "results" have fueled the dropout problem. Across the nation, under 70% of the students entering high schools will graduate on time.[3] The problem is worse for minority students in urban areas and in the south, where from 50 to 60% of ninth-graders will not graduate on time.[4]

The current political winds are blowing away from cultivating the educational opportunities necessary for strengthening what Richard Florida calls the "creative class,"[5] toward policies of standardizing schooling and emphasizing the kinds of accountability practices that can paralyze risk-taking. Public schools will need to explore new practices in order to retain the interest of children and parents and to prepare a creative class that can meet the challenges of a global economy.

This emphasis on standards runs very much against the grain of the technological imperatives of customization, interaction, and learner control. To cope with these imperatives, schools need to embody more individual support and choice in how and what students learn. They will need to engage students in more challenging and realistic tasks that reflect the uses of knowledge in the world. The activities will need to be much more engaging and interactive than what passes for school activities currently. The tasks will need to make sense to students and will need to be more oriented to the students' long-term goals and interests. These imperatives have strong implications for the design of curriculum, assessment, and equity.

Kids today spend over 6 hours per day interacting with television, video games, the Internet, instant messaging, email, and other media.[6] This is more time than they spend in school or with friends, and almost as much time as they spend sleeping. As we have seen in previous chapters, education entrepreneurs are developing new methods for linking the worlds of media and learning. Here, we propose several areas for policy development to help public schools take similar advantage of new telecommunications media. Hopefully, initiatives in these directions will help public schools participate in, rather than resist, the ongoing educational revolution.

We do not need to start a new education system from scratch. Designing a better education system means understanding where the existing pieces can best be reshaped, brought together, or played down. In this chapter, we discuss three areas that might help bring together the best of the old and the new: performance-based assessment, new curriculum designs, and new approaches to equity in a digital world.

PERFORMANCE-BASED ASSESSMENT

The national obsession with standardized testing has led some researchers to pursue new understandings of how to measure learning. We would like to highlight two aspects of this recent work: national certifications and skill-based assessment systems.

One way to bring together established and new approaches to learning would be to develop a set of national credentials that could be administered on computer or by trained professionals at any school or learning center. People would be able to apply for as many credential certifications as they like and take the exams for them whenever they feel they are ready. This differs from school, where exams are administered when the teacher or district decides. These credentials would be much more narrowly focused than a high school diploma. Instead of institutional certifications, as with diplomas or degrees, these credentials would certify a learner's expertise with respect to specific skills.

By tying certifications to the specific goals of learners and their parents, assessment could be much more attuned to the technological imperatives of customization and learner control. If a student's goal is to become a doctor, he or she might need to get certificates to demonstrate expertise in chemistry, biology, psychology, college-level literacy and math skills, and so on. If a student wants to become a travel agent, he or she will need to establish expertise in reading, listening, explaining, geography, psychology, resource management, scheduling, and so forth. There would need to be an online system that parents and students could consult to learn which certificates are needed for different career choices, what needs to be known in order to obtain each certificate, and what methods might be used to obtain the necessary knowledge.

We see the certifications as being developed in three areas: academic skills, generic skills, and technical skills. In the academic area, there might be an English competency certificate at different grade levels of reading and writing competency, and certification exams in history, math, languages, science, the arts, and other school disciplines. Getting a certain credential would, like the current diploma system, allow students to move on to the next level of schooling. If people wanted to take courses to prepare for the exams, they could do so, or if they wanted to study on their own, they could do that. Some people might obtain a large number of these credentials, and some might obtain fewer credentials.

The generic skills certifications would follow the general guidelines of the Department of Labor's SCANS report.[7] The report suggests five competency areas: resource allocation, working with others, acquiring and using information, understanding complex systems, and working with a variety of technologies. Within each area, there might be a number of different credentials. Technical skills would be focused on specific skills required for the workplace, such as automotive diagnosis, CAD-CAM design, and so on. Students would choose which certificates they want to earn, and they would know in advance how their performance in carrying out the assessment tasks would be judged.

The choice of credentials they try for would be up to the students and their parents, and would depend on their career interests and plans. Of course, one problem with a credentialing system would be for students who do not know exactly which educational path to take. In this new educational world, most children would continue with the kinds of elementary schools and middle schools they now attend to make sure they had experience with different kinds of students and teachers, and could envision different educational paths. The internal organization of these schools, however, would be organized around credentialing requirements rather than specific courses based on Carnegie units. At the next level, students would continue to take a series of required credentialing programs, but would have increasing autonomy to select their preferred credentials. In order to help them make these decisions, they should have access to a multimedia advisory system to learn about the sorts of credentials that are valued by employers in different job categories, businesses, and professions.

So far, this design sounds like the current high school requirement and electives design, except that students would decide when they are ready to take an exam. Everything would depend upon the integrity of the certification system for credentialing. Ensuring the integrity of the certification system would require content experts to agree on what is worth knowing. The certification standard process would build on the already robust subject-matter standards discussions of the National Council of Teachers of Mathematics or the Advanced Placement programs. The conversations about what is worth knowing and certifying could draw out areas of agreement between school- and technology-based teachers and point to how the national standards movement could describe what students actually need to know and do as a result of their educational experiences.

Computers are revolutionizing how we measure what people know. Computer adaptive testing systems use a test-taker's prior answers to select which items would best measure what the student knows. If a student fails to answer a question, the system provides an easier question; if the student is successful, he or she receives a more difficult question. Currently used for exams such as the Graduate Record Exam (GRE) and the Test of English as a Foreign Language (TOEFL), computer adaptive testing technologies open up a range of assessment uses that could link old and new approaches to schooling and learning.

Computer-based testing will also help capture the kinds of knowledge and skills required for learning in the professions. These assessments allow researchers to specify and measure the kinds of professional knowledge that had previously only been observable through performance. Robert Mislevy's work on evidence-centered assessment shows how assessments can be designed around sophisticated models of expert knowledge, and can be used to measure what professionals such as dental hygienists need to know and do.[8] These evidence-based assessments link the knowledge to be assessed, the behaviors that demonstrate knowledge, and the tasks that elicit the behaviors into a computer adaptive testing system. The underlying knowledge models from Mislevy's assessment systems are complex and difficult to construct, but they point to how measures of the skills and knowledge developed in K–12 schooling can be extended to capture professional knowledge.

Evidence-centered assessments can also be used together with certification systems to focus educational discussion on the outcomes of learning. Assessment activities could then be more like authentic tasks developed by knowledgeable members of the educational, business, and assessment communities. Students could attempt to earn credentials as many times as they would like, and the evaluators in the assessment centers would have the responsibility of helping students understand the strengths and weaknesses of their performance and how they might improve in their next attempt at earning the credential. Earning a credential would provide students with an opportunity to have their accomplishments recognized by knowledgeable professionals, and evaluated according to standards that are accepted by that community.

Students would create a portfolio of credentials for purposes of employment or college applications. Unlike current high school and college diploma certifications, the performance-based certification system would be linked to the kinds of knowledge and skills that matter for adult learning. Developing a performance-based certification system would also force educators to be more careful about defining what they expect students to know and do.

NEW CURRICULUM DESIGNS

Computer technologies open new avenues for curriculum development—ranging from new forms of teaching and learning to new ways of organizing how students and teachers interact. One curriculum design that we favor is using technology to help students focus their learning around their goals and interests. Such schools would place students in curricula based on their goals and interests, rather than on their ages or on the prevailing curriculum of their schools.[9] The curriculum might start off in the early years with topics such as families, ecology, sports, or dinosaurs, and progress to areas such as film-making and media production, biomedicine, or business management. Traditional academic skills, such as reading, writing, mathematics, science, history, and geography, would be woven into each curriculum.

Students would be encouraged to stick with a particular curriculum for a long time, perhaps several years, while they develop deep skills and understanding. Each child, with the help of their parents, would choose one or two curricula to start with, but might change from one curriculum to another, with the agreement of the teachers and parents. As children advance, they would move into curricula that reflect the kinds of things adults do in the world, such as learning about the arts, business, or technology. But they should not change curricula frequently or they will never develop deep skills and knowledge in any domain.

Such a curriculum emphasizes students learning important content and skills in the context of carrying out complex tasks, such as making a video about the evolution of dinosaurs. We have developed a four-stage model for student learning in this kind of curriculum that reflects how apprenticeship works in a large shop: 1) Students come in as novices and work on a small project of their own with one of the more experienced students mentoring them, as they carry out the project; 2) As they gain experience, they begin to work on larger projects with other students, where more advanced students serve as project and subproject leaders; 3) After they have worked on a number of different projects, they are ready to serve as a mentor for a new incoming student; 4) After they successfully mentor new students, they are ready to begin serving as a project or subproject leader on larger projects.

When students become teenagers, we would trust them to follow a number of different paths. They might attend school, work, study at home to take certificate exams, or participate in some kind of youth organization, such as AmeriCorps. If they want to go to college, they might try to get all the certifications they need for college as soon as possible. Hence, some might go off to college at age 15 or 16. Others might work for a while and then come back to school to prepare for college. Ideally, the state would pay for student's education to prepare for a certain number of certificates (perhaps 20 or 30). Then people could take courses whenever they are ready, at whatever age. Developing policies that encourage a mixed-age population in courses, filled with people who have chosen to be there, might well alleviate some of the current problems with motivating students to participate in high school.

In the high school years, David Shaffer's design for future schools organizes learning around professional practices.[10] Shaffer argues that school curricula are currently organized around antiquated forms of thought that make it difficult for students to link what they learn to what they will do later in life. Professions, such as journalism, urban planning, and engineering, have organized knowledge, beliefs, values, and strategies into what Shaffer calls *epistemic frames*. These frames have been refined over time, and offer well-honed models for integrating knowing and doing. Game-based learning technologies can play a key role in introducing students to epistemic frames. In the urban planning curriculum, for example, Shaffer and his research group developed an interactive tool that allows students to represent and manipulate buildings, parks, sanitation, and parking space. The tool is grounded in the real practices of urban planners, and is embedded in a curriculum designed to help students make predictions, experiment with their solutions, and face political heat for their decisions. Together, the tool and the curriculum provide an excellent introduction to the political, financial, and architectural dimensions of urban planning. Using established professions as the basis for curriculum design allows Shaffer to explore how students can learn math, history, science, and politics connected to authentic contexts.

Other approaches to fitting learning technologies into schools could focus on the topics schools have typically had difficulty teaching, such as scientific investigation or historical and ecological systems. The Center for Learning Technologies in Urban Schools (LeTUS) was one of many National Science Foundation–funded efforts to develop project-based science curricula for urban K–12 schools. LeTUS developed sophisticated computer-based visualization and analysis tools for students to investigate topics such as air and water quality, global warming, and plate tectonics. The LeTUS developers were not content to build curriculum and see whether the teachers were interested. Rather, LeTUS used a client-focused approach to development that involved teachers and researchers in lesson design teams, and consulted for urban district technology and curriculum leaders to make project-based science part of the regular science program. Although an emphasis on reading and math scores has, in recent years, dominated the instructional agenda for most urban school districts, projects like LeTUS illustrate how schools and researchers together can integrate technologies into everyday school learning.

Commercial video games can also be adapted to meet content standards in schools. Games such as *Civilization* build on models of historical progress and conflict, allowing players to see how cultures that develop religious, military, economic, or diplomatic superiority can influence the course of world development. After playing such games, students should reflect as a class on the historical implications of the events as they unfolded. In particular, they should try to relate what happened to events they have read about in books and seen in videos of historical events, such as World War II. This glimpse into the process of how history unfolds is lacking in most textbook-dominated, fact-based approaches to history learning in schools. Helping teachers understand how system-modeling games like *Civilization*, *Railroad Tycoon*, and *The Sims* could help students better meet content goals could serve to introduce learning technologies into everyday school practices.

Outside the realm of standards-based subject matter, games can also help students develop interpersonal and leadership skills. Massively multiplayer online games, such as *World of Warcraft*, allow players to solve complex problems involving strategy, logistics, and resource allocation. In MMOGs, players interact with social groups to recruit and retain new members, coordinate large-scale movements, and make decisions about political values. Games like *SWAT 4* and the U.S. Army's *Full Spectrum Warrior* also give players a chance to develop tactical and leadership skills, leading John Seely Brown and Douglas Thomas to suggest that video games may well be the environments that train the next generation of business leaders.[11]

A final point about how technologies could affect schooling involves course management systems. Many colleges and universities use systems from companies such as Blackboard and Desire2Learn for online access to discussion boards, collaborative project development spaces, and online textbooks and readings. Although technically these systems only organize the content developed by teachers and students, the communication tools provided can open up spaces for alternative discussion. Teachers or students can use the discussion boards, for example, to explore some of the difficult readings, or to engage in group design for course projects. More important, students who find it difficult to participate in class discussions can use the online discussions to interact and get to know their classmates.

Course management systems integrate the kinds of communication technologies used outside of school into typical course content. Although K–12 schools have been slower to adopt course management tools, K–12 students accustomed to instant messaging and MySpace.com will quickly recognize how course management systems can open up new opportunities for interaction. Using course management systems for basic K–12 courses will help integrate communication technologies into the core of existing school programs.

NEW APPROACHES TO EQUITY IN A DIGITAL WORLD

Schools must face the challenge of harnessing the power of learning technologies at the same time as the pendulum of education policy is swinging away from creativity toward policies based on standardizing schooling and emphasizing the kinds of accountability practices that paralyze risk-taking. In an effort to provide equality of outcomes, federal and state policies informed by the No Child Left Behind Act have shifted educational practice toward pervasive acceptance of "what works"—reductive, teacher-proof curricula that produce similar learning outcomes across all schools.

The short-term effects of these policies hurt public school families from both ends of the economic scale: Standardized curricula drive affluent families from public schools, and high dropout rates push poor families to press for alternatives to public schools. Technology-based learning venues, from home schools to virtual charters to learning centers, allow families to opt out of the public system in order to support their religious or ideological approach to education. Learning technologies, it seems, are mainly used to increase the inequity of opportunities. How can learning technologies be used to address the systemic inequities of public schools?

We feel that, in addition to the curricular ideas described above, learning technologies can address the inequity of educational opportunity through offering new, technologically mediated educational experiences to poor schools and developing technology-based systems for tracking what students are learning in schools. Writers such as Jonathan Kozol paint a bleak picture of how many urban students, despite living in thriving cities, rarely travel from their own neighborhoods, and become trapped by the impoverished academic fare that dominates their classrooms.[12] Learning technologies may not be able to address the underlying economic distress that limits how students can travel outside their homes, but they can bring high-quality academic experiences into local schools.

The College Board's Advanced Placement (AP) program, for example, has proven to be one of the few educational innovations that has successfully "gone to scale." High school students from around the country take Advanced Placement courses in literature, the social and natural sciences, mathematics, and other subjects that are graded on a common scale by external evaluators to ensure common outcomes. Still, it is difficult for many schools to offer a wide range of AP classes because of staff commitments and lack of student interest. The drastic cost reduction of video teleconferencing makes shared access to AP courses through distance education a ready option for many poor urban and rural schools. Organizations such as the Florida Virtual School increasingly act as brokers for providing courses that local schools are unable to offer.[13]

Virtual tutoring is another example of how technology can add to a school's academic resources. Tutoring for students who struggle is an often overlooked, and criticized, feature of the No Child Left Behind Act. Critics contend that the federal call for tutoring undercuts school efforts to teach by diverting millions of dollars to private companies whose tutors are not held to the same standards as teachers.[14] Still, the government call for tutoring can be seen as a new bridge from the existing to the emerging worlds of learning. Virtual tutoring, in particular, may provide an important path for connecting students in struggling schools with the outside world. A recent *Time* magazine article discussed how companies such as the India-based TutorVista offer competitive rates in K–12 tutoring for "everything from grammar to geometry."[15] All the arguments in the current debate over outsourcing knowledge work certainly apply here; communication technologies make it possible to deepen the linkage between the continents and shrink the world to meet even the most personal needs for teaching and learning.

We return to the issue of how to use technologies to address problems of equity in Chapter 10. Clearly, technology has exacerbated the problem of equity in education, and we need to think carefully about how we can mitigate the problem.

9

What Does It All Mean?

The future is already here, it's just unevenly distributed.
—William Gibson[1]

The consequences of the current educational revolution are just beginning to be felt. Technology-driven venues for learning are springing up everywhere, and technological innovations are having unanticipated influence outside of the public school system. Our brief tour in Chapter 4 through the evolution of public schooling in America showed how we came to identify "learning" with formal schooling. New technologies are beginning to unravel this common sense definition.

John Hagel and John Seely Brown argue that successful businesses need to learn from innovations at the edges of their markets. In times of rapid market changes, they comment that "If we adjust our lenses accordingly, then we will begin to see something remarkable: The edges will reshape and eventually transform the core."[2] For the "edges" to reform the core of schooling, we will have to become both intelligent consumers and producers of the next generation of learning technologies.

Even those of us who don't embrace technology in our lives now must understand the *possibilities* of the new technologies from the inside, if we want to guide the future of education. As Don Tapscott argues "For the first time in history, children are more comfortable, knowledgeable, and literate than their parents about an innovation central to society. . . . They are a force for social transformation."[3] In this chapter, we offer suggestions for parents and teachers on how to bridge the considerable generation gap and integrate new learning technologies into existing practices.

WHAT ARE KIDS LEARNING FROM TECHNOLOGY?

The emergence of technology-based learning environments requires parents and teachers to pay attention to how (and what) children learn outside of school and the home. Beyond raising awareness of the new technologies, parents and teachers can begin to appreciate the range of new skills that children develop when immersed in these technologies.

The technology literacy gap begins at home. Although parents provide their children with access to television, games, computers, instant messaging, and cell phones, many confess that they do not really understand how children use the new technologies. Video games provide the clearest case of the technology generation gap. Many parents (and school leaders) frame the "problem" of video games in terms of addiction and the "corruption of our youth." They rightly worry that many of the games in which children are engaged are violent and that kids are wasting a lot of time in meaningless games and idle talk, while not getting enough physical exercise.

Meanwhile, children who play video games develop sophisticated problem-solving and communication skills in virtual worlds beyond the experience of many parents. One way to bridge the gap is to extend the idea of reading with your children to playing with your children. Pick up a controller and take *Madden 2005* or *Pokemon* for a ride; let your children teach you how to play, and raise critical questions about strategies and the purpose of game-play. If your child uses instant messaging on her phone or computer, sign up for an account and use it as a medium for communication.

Another direction parents can pursue is to encourage their children to join online communities that share their deep interests. Different kids may have a passion for dinosaurs, poetry, sports, drawing, astronomy, horses, military history, technology, and so forth. Whatever their interests may be, extended pursuit of these interests can develop expertise that may be highly valuable in later life. It may also develop their research skills, which can be valuable in many endeavors throughout their lives. We think parents might try to set up groups of children of different ages around those topics that particular children are passionate about. They would then be able to share their passions with a group of like-minded children. This would encourage them to learn about their passion much more deeply than they can on their own. Often, children cannot find others locally who share their passions, but the reach of the Internet would allow them to go beyond their neighborhood and school to find like-minded children.

For example, children might pursue a passion for dinosaurs in a Multi-User Virtual Environment (or MUVE), such as Second Life. A MUVE allows children to construct places using text descriptions or drawing programs.

As we mentioned in Chapter 5, a student on his own time created a simulated rain forest in MicroMuse, an educational MUVE. Similarly, children might construct various exhibits in a MUVE: One exhibit might be a dinosaur zoo where they lay out the dimensions of areas to support different dinosaurs and write vivid descriptions of the dinosaurs, flora, and fauna that populate the areas in the zoo. Another might have a timeline of the history of the Earth, showing when different dinosaurs lived, when they died out, and when humans arrived on the scene. A third might have a simulated world where children can search for dinosaur bones hidden in places where they have been found historically. There also might be a forum discussing the evidence for different theories of why the dinosaurs died out or whether birds have descended from dinosaurs. Children would be learning reading, writing, drawing, geometry, arithmetic, history, geography, biology, and paleontology, all in the context of their passion.

The virtue of communities of kids with shared passions is that they can take place without any involvement of schools and with little adult involvement. If adult mentors do participate in the groups, they should probably keep to the background while encouraging the children to go in new directions that they might not explore on their own. Because the online communities tap into children's passions, they should be self-sustaining, and the community will encourage children to learn deeply about a subject they care about. If you question how your child learning about dinosaurs in a MUVE will help him or her get a "real job," consider for example how a group of 11-year-olds in California we know, who became passionate about developing Internet games, formed a corporation to sell their games over the Internet. Society values such entrepreneurial drive, as well as deep expertise in a subject area.

A common concern expressed by parents and teachers is that time online equals more time that kids aren't reading books. Literacy researchers have long recognized the importance of the early development of rich, functional vocabularies to fuel language development. While solitary reading has always been a steady, gradual path to a larger vocabulary, talking about what you read with people who have larger vocabularies greatly accelerates development. James Paul Gee, an educational linguist, suggests that video games such as *Deus Ex* can provide engines for vocabulary development.[4] Just as with reading, however, the games themselves provide slow vocabulary acquisition. But when players participate in a larger gaming community, games can accelerate opportunities for children to develop new sources of vocabulary in meaningful contexts.

It is difficult to predict how the new technologies will affect more advanced literacy skills, such as finding information and interpreting visual representations. Policymakers interested in preparing students for success in the 21st-century economy would do well, however, to appreciate how skills developed through navigating virtual environments might pay off in the workplace. In *Got Game*, John C. Beck and Mitchell Wade suggest that the new skills and dispositions of the gamer generation will transform the workplace.[5] The gamer generation will push for work environments to incorporate more virtual aspects in fields, such as market analysis, and social and economic modeling. Gamers, for example, have abundant experience making big decisions, coordinating resources, and experimenting with complex strategies in game-based simulations. Beck and Wade also note how gamers have become accustomed to being rewarded for success across multiple game-based environments. This may create pay-for-performance expectations, and may make gamers less loyal to companies and more willing to shift to jobs where there are greater challenges. Although Beck and Wade's work is attempting to map uncharted territory, it is already clear that the work world of tomorrow will be shaped in part by the gaming technologies of today.

HOW HAS TECHNOLOGY CHANGED KIDS' SOCIAL LIVES AND LEARNING?

The convergence of peer and popular culture through technologies presents possibly the largest threat (and opportunity) for schools and parents. As discussed in Chapter 6, the rise of high schools in the mid-20th century provided the conditions for the emergence of a vibrant peer culture among teens. Beginning in the 1950s, advertisers began to cultivate the lucrative market of teens with disposable income to create pop culture focused on customizing music, style, sports, and movies for teen audiences. Youth participation in pop culture provided a compelling alternative to the social experience of schooling as organized by adults—by the 1960s, millions of teens went to school primarily to associate with friends rather than to get an education. Entertainment technologies fueled the development of pop culture—record players, radios, TVs, and eight–track car stereos are the clear precedents for cell phones, PCs, and iPods. The adolescent (and now pre-adolescent) embrace of the new technologies has reinforced peer cultures through the development of new jargon, from hip-hop slang to instant-messaging conventions, that make the technologies more desirable by promising exclusivity to those in the know.

In recent years, American peer culture itself became a powerful economic engine, generating thousands of jobs and millions of dollars around the world. In fact, pop culture, in the form of music, sports, style, movies, and video games, now provides some of America's leading exports. The explosion of American pop culture displays the fundamental signature of an information economy to generate goods and services, not through the previously dominant method of harnessing raw materials, but instead through the packaging and marketing of human resources as valuable commodities in their own right. In this sense, the pop culture industry prefigured the computing boom of the 1980s and 1990s by generating an immense industry from attractive ideas rather than from resources dug from the earth.

The titans of the entertainment industry are currently locked in battle with Internet upstarts on issues around digital distribution and ownership. But the battle over who controls the media may take a back seat to the role of participation in new forms of entertainment. If pop culture can generate substantial economic growth around the world, how will familiarity with pop culture pay off? In other words, will all those evenings watching television or playing Nintendo turn into good jobs?

Steven Johnson suggests that the recent content of the media is advancing a new, cognitively demanding form of participatory media literacy right before our eyes.[6] Television shows such as *24* and *Lost* involve multiple narrative threads that unfold across episodes, while reality shows break the traditional narrative paths open by allowing participants to determine the narrative arc. Viewers create web sites just to follow along with the show, as well as to discuss plot twists and favorite characters. The video game rests at the top of the cognitive complexity chart, as players must solve complex problems using a variety of strategies over the course of dozens or even hundreds of hours to complete the game. As the information economy continues its turn toward the production of virtual environments, experience with the nuances of the new media might lead to informed production as well as informed consumption. Blogging has certainly been taken seriously by established news networks, and we will see whether the entertainment industry will be revolutionized by participatory media or will succeed in reducing the new media to current forms of production and control.

WHERE DOES THIS LEAVE US?

We advise the technological skeptics that they might be looking in the wrong place for change in the core practices of schools. Researchers such as Larry Cuban have looked for, and have not found, the influence of technological innovation in the classroom. Instead, technological innovation is breaking out in the administrative office with data systems and among students with gaming, leaving the teachers behind to maintain their traditional classroom practices.

The pressure to change the classroom with computing is coming from outside the classroom, in different forms from children and families and the central office. To be sure, the trivial implementation of new technologies as supplements to the existing system will continue—there will still be plenty of math homework web sites. But the funneling of state money into charter schools and federal money into tutorial services will challenge our schools to do business in new ways in order to take advantage of increasingly scarce new funding streams. Whether schools change internally or become parts of larger public-private networks of educational services, we suspect that schools will be dragged reluctantly into a new technologically rich education system.

The new system, unfortunately, will probably not mark a victory for technology enthusiasts, even though the development of a low-cost, robust computer for the world's poor may empower a whole new generation of kids. Enthusiasts who anticipate the natural emergence of change in schools would do well to study the existing structures of schooling to identify the aspects of the current system that are ripe for innovation.

This is the time for technological visionaries to act. We are now at the same stage in the second educational revolution that we were in during the last decades of the 19th century. The central pieces of the emerging system—kindergarten, high schools, graded curriculum, textbooks—were already in existence and beginning to coalesce into a new system. It took a strong local push in districts like St. Louis, New York, and Boston, together with an emerging new field of study in educational administration and psychology, to fit these pieces together into the "one-best system." Now we face a similar swirl of new pieces of a potential system—virtual charters, learning centers, video games, home schooling, and so on. We need strong leadership from innovative educators to make sure that the new system embodies our society's critical goals for education.

10

Rethinking Education in
a Technological World

We argue for a new vision of education. To be successful, political and educational leaders will need to carefully consider the changes in our society and mobilize the government's resources to address the problems we've raised and to achieve the great potential ahead of us.

Since the end of World War II, the United States has enjoyed a disproportionate share of global resources. This abundance allowed Americans to maintain a high standard of living and take a world leadership role. Thomas Friedman's "the world is flat" argument suggests that access to information technologies has leveled the global playing field.[1] This leveling is allowing millions of engineers, technologists, and professionals from around the world to pursue the careers that have made so many Americans wealthy. The future prosperity of countries around the world depends on how their education systems can be designed to foster economic development. If the United States is going to compete successfully in a global economy, it will have to rethink many of its assumptions about education.

The formula for economic success has a high cost. As has happened in the United States, countries that focus on knowledge economies as the source of wealth generation tend to concentrate economic resources on an elite class. The gap between the haves and have nots is growing, not shrinking, in many developed countries, and focusing the national commitment in education toward elite populations motivated to participate in math, science, and technology careers might further widen the gap. Global competition might spark what W. E. B. DuBois called a "top 10%" education strategy that will concentrate resources and push the most talented students toward globally competitive professions. Writers such as Gary Orfield and Chungmei Lee suggest that resegregation of schools and communities, voucher policies, and charter schools are already pushing our education policy away from its commitment to equity.[2]

Just how technological developments will help us balance the goals of equity and global competition is not yet clear. The rethinking of education that we promote with this book should aim toward strategies that provide access to the new educational resources for everyone in society, and give people the motivation to take advantage of these resources. This demands rethinking education not in isolation, but considering the interplay of society, education, and learning.

RETHINKING LEARNING

We grew up with the idea that learning means taking courses in school. As we argued throughout this book, the identification of education with schooling is slowly unraveling, as new technologies move learning outside of school's walls. In some sense, the divorce of schooling and learning may take us back to an era where individuals negotiate their own learning experiences, often with strong guidance from their parents.

Eventually, when people and politicians become worried about what kids are learning or what adults don't know, their automatic reaction may not be "How can we improve the schools?". Instead, they may ask, "How can we develop games to teach history?", "How can we make new technology resources available to more people?", or "What kinds of tools can support people to seek out information on their own?". Currently, the strong association between schooling and learning forces our conversation into institutional responses. We don't yet know how to ask these wider questions when we think about improving education. We hope this book starts that conversation.

As learning moves out of school, our conception of learning will begin to broaden, and we will see more hybrid experiences that begin in the classroom and move into other contexts. Education may follow the path of home schooling by emphasizing field trips, interacting with peers, playing computer games, or even teaching others with technological tools. For example, a teacher who taught computer programming was approached by a few of his students who wanted to bring their own computers into the school and hook them up in a network to engage in multiplayer games with one another. They asked to form a computer club where they would begin to develop computer games of their own. As new kids joined the club, the first group would teach them some of the things they themselves had learned. Later, when the teacher was given the task of setting up a network in a nearby school, the kids helped him with the design and implementation of the network, and with getting students in the other school working with their new network. Although all this learning took place in a school setting, it was not "real school" learning. Technology directors around the country are experimenting with similar models that rely on students to provide network design and support.

Our vision of education in this book is structured around the idea of *lifelong learning*. Lifelong learning requires moving away from highly structured schooling institutions to instead act as consumers of a wide variety of learning experiences. Learners will need to develop the skills to judge the quality of learning venues and the kinds of social networks that provide guidance and advice.

Brigid Barron provides a good example of how students learn to become intelligent consumers of learning environments through developing their computer skills.[3] For example, one middle school girl in California named Stephanie, who was the daughter of Chinese immigrants, had a group of friends who used GeoCities to create their own web pages. They taught Stephanie how to use HTML, which appealed to her since she liked to draw. Then, in seventh grade, she took courses in programming, web design, and industrial technology, where she used a computer to do designs. In eighth grade, she decided to develop a web page for her family and helped her father design a web page for his new business. She even taught her mother different ways to use computers. As she got further into art with the computer, she lurked in the background of Xanga, an online digital-art community, trying to pick up techniques for making computer art. She would study the finished works and the source code that the artists used to produce their works. She is a typical self-directed learner in the digital age.

The recent explosion of social networking points to how technologies can replicate the support and guidance functions of schools. These networks draw people across all ages from very different backgrounds, some quite expert and others virtual novices. Some learn by lurking in the background and others by asking questions. Groups in the network may jointly investigate topics of interest or argue about issues they consider important. The successful sites, however, share the characteristic of providing useful information to guide the interests of users. For example, user groups and community sites exist for every known disease and disorder, and doctors across the country know their diagnoses are checked by an increasingly informed patient population. These kinds of social networks are blossoming around topics of particular interest to different groups of people, topics such as poetry, chemistry, digital graphics, and fantasy sports. Reliable information sites, such as homework.com, tutor.com, and collegeboard.com, are already supplanting the guidance departments, financial aid centers, and even the tutoring and homework services that are provided as common staples of institutional schooling.

What might happen if our thinking about learning doesn't change? If schools cannot change fast enough to keep pace with advances in learning technologies, learning will leave schooling behind. We see this happening outside of the United States already. For example, with inexpensive computers, young people in Thailand and Brazil can have access to the same resources for learning that people in the developed world now have. Many will choose to take advantage of these resources to escape from poverty. In some ways, they will be a new kind of 21st-century immigrant—instead of moving to a new country, they will use information networks to transform their thinking. They will be able to find like-minded souls to share ideas in cyberspace. English will likely be their common language, which they will pick up from the web.

As older generations continue to impose established methods of learning in school, technologies will leech critical learning resources, such as student motivation, attention, and resources, out of the education system. Trying to reassert the identification of schooling and learning will be a losing battle.

RETHINKING MOTIVATION

The current school system does not help students develop intrinsic motivation to learn. The disengagement experienced by many students is reinforced by less-than-ideal classroom experiences. One recent report found that 50% of high school students are bored every day in their classes; another found that 82% of California 9th- and 10th-graders reported their school experiences as "boring and irrelevant."[4] Changing these deeply ingrained attitudes about learning will mean changing both the process of teaching and learning and the reward system for successful completion of schooling.

Fortunately, learning technologies provide some direction about how to improve student motivation to learn and to invigorate learning content.

In order to produce a generation of people who seek out learning, learners need to be given more control over their own learning. Learner control can be fostered by giving kids the tools to support their own learning, such as access to the web, machines for toddlers that teach reading, tutoring help when needed, and computer-based games that foster deep knowledge and entrepreneurial skills.

A love of learning can also be fostered by encouraging kids to explore deeply topics in which they are particularly interested, as home-schooling parents do. As Kurt Squire found, kids who play real-time strategy games, such as *Civilization*, begin to check out books on ancient cultures and earn better grades in middle school.[5] Instead of diverting student attention from schools, as feared by many teachers and school leaders, video games can provide a path to make conventional school content more appealing and encourage students to give their classroom instruction another chance. By understanding how new technologies can encourage kids to take responsibility for their own learning, society may help produce a generation of people who seek out ways to learn.

Pushing students to take more control of their learning, as we have discussed, runs counter to the institutional control of learning exercised by schools. Fostering self-learning will require challenging the current policy assumptions that press schools to teach everyone the same thing at the same time. Even the one-room schools that preceded universal schooling resisted this contemporary impulse to standardize instruction. Integrating computers into the center of schooling, rather than at the periphery, could help learners pursue individualized, interactive lessons with adequate support. Such systems can control the level of challenge by choosing tasks that reflect the learner's recent history. Teachers can help out when students need more assistance than the computer can provide. Such individualized learning would remove the stigma of looking bad when you don't understand something that others grasp.

Technologies also point to another path toward fostering a love of learning through design and production. Savvy computer game developers have long realized how including design tools to alter the game environment greatly increases the replay value and brand loyalty of their games. Giving students meaningful tasks to accomplish will help them understand why they are doing what they are doing. Students who struggle in school spend hundreds of hours tweaking football rosters to meet salary cap requirements in *Madden* or editing parody videos on YouTube. Suddenly, when the drudge work of complicated tasks becomes contextualized and has new significance, students are more than willing to take the time to "get it right." As a society, we need to understand how new technologies turn kids and adults on to learning, in order to redesign our learning environments to provide positive motivational experiences for all learners.

RETHINKING WHAT IS IMPORTANT TO LEARN

Of course, providing intrinsic motivation to learn also requires us to rethink the rewards of successfully completing a course of learning. There is a mismatch between the programs that schools offer and the kinds of skills that are needed to live a successful life in a knowledge economy. The core curriculum in modern schools is still rooted in the medieval *trivium* (from which the word *trivial* is derived), which consisted of logic, grammar, and rhetoric, and *quadrivium*, which was made up of arithmetic, geometry, music, and astronomy. These formed the bases for the liberal arts, which dominate the current course of study in school and college. Over the centuries, we added courses such as history, geography, and the sciences, but the basic organization of the curriculum reflects its historical roots.

A question that society must wrestle with is whether this is the best curriculum for preparing students to live in an age with rich technological resources. Proponents of traditional curricula argue that classical training in thinking and writing is needed now more than ever; progressive educators suggest that new literacy skills and mathematical reasoning skills are needed for new times. In schools, however, the compromise between the two camps is often to organize content roughly in classical disciplines, but to remove the rigor and the context from the classical content. Thus, geometry is presented without a sense of history, and sciences are learned as sets of facts instead of methods to organize observations and experiments. Because we think of education as what goes on in school, this compromise curriculum furnishes a narrow and quite impoverished view of what is important to learn.

There are two areas in which the new technological resources clearly impact what is important to learn: communication and mathematics. In 21st-century communication practices, boundaries are becoming blurred between core literacy practices, such as learning to read and write, and more applied production and presentation practices. Creating multimedia documents, putting together and critiquing videos, finding information and resources on the web, and understanding images and graphics are all becoming important aspects of communication. New technologies offer interesting ways to make the transition between basic and applied literacies. For example, the people who play massively multiplayer online games (MMOGs), such as *World of Warcraft* or *Lineage*, use basic literacy practices to develop a whole range of other applied literacy skills, such as negotiation, bargaining, forming alliances, strategizing and outwitting opponents, calculating which approach is most likely to work, and communicating with different kinds of people. These applied literacy skills occur naturally in MMOGs but are difficult to maintain in traditional school environments. Yet, because we think of literacy skill development as being directly tied to traditional school content, most people regard gamers as wasting their time playing these multiplayer games.

.In terms of mathematics, technology can carry out all of the algorithms that students spend so much time learning in school. At the same time, learning to think mathematically is more important than ever. Therefore, students' time might be better spent in learning how to use mathematical tools to solve real-world problems, rather than learning how to mimic computer algorithms. In fact, understanding how to apply computer tools appropriately requires much more thinking than executing algorithms. It should become the new agenda for teaching mathematics. Fantasy sports present a case in point for teaching applied mathematical skills. Calculating on-base percentages or adding up runs scored may not involve sophisticated algorithmic processes, but even the most casual fantasy baseball player must engage in predictive models to anticipate which players and teams have the best chance to succeed. Having fantasy players articulate their predictive models is an excellent exercise in developing the kinds of estimation and number sense skills prized by organizations such as the National Council of Teachers of Mathematics.

A subtle impact of technology on learning has to do with the easy availability of knowledge on the web. In the past, people have had to memorize a lot of information in order to make competent decisions, as doctors must do to make accurate diagnoses. But with easy access to knowledge, people can rely more on external memories to help them out. We can illustrate this phenomenon with the use of technology by doctors. Online systems have been developed in recent years that help doctors make diagnoses. Doctors can feed the systems with sets of symptoms, and the systems can suggest possible diagnoses that the doctors should consider. That way, the doctor does not have to remember every possible pairing of symptoms to diagnoses. Doctors still must apply their personal knowledge, gained from experience and from interaction with the patient, in order to make their decisions. These systems act essentially as memory aids. Similarly, the web is a huge memory aid, in addition to providing new information on every topic under the sun. The essential skill is no longer memorization, but knowing how to find the information you want on the web, including how to evaluate what you find, given the differences in reliability among web sites. That is to say, people need to develop new learning skills rather than acquiring more information.

One approach to a new specification of what students need to know is provided by a Harlem high school.[6] The school stresses that the students should learn to ask and answer reflective questions that correspond to five Habits of Mind: 1) From what viewpoint are we seeing, reading, or hearing this?; 2) How do we know what we know? What's the evidence, and how reliable is it?; 3) How are things, events, or people connected? What is the cause and effect? How do they fit?; 4) What if . . .? Could things be otherwise? What are or were the alternatives?; 5) So what? Why does it matter? What does it all mean? Who cares? These questions are central to everything the students do in the school, and even in the evaluation of students to determine if they have learned enough to graduate. These questions stretch the definition of what is taught in a school to encompass the types of thinking and action required for adaptive thinking in an information-rich world.

RETHINKING CAREERS

While education has traditionally aimed to enlighten learners about their political responsibilities, American discussions of education have recently turned sharply toward career preparation for economic success. But as routine jobs are replaced by technology or shipped offshore, the remaining jobs emphasize collaboration, communication, and knowledge-processing skills. From an economic perspective, it's imperative for education to focus much more on teaching students how to think critically in a digital age, and how to find the knowledge and resources they need to accomplish difficult tasks. Students would be much better served if they were challenged to solve real-world problems and create meaningful products. Then they might have some incentive to learn how to think.

Career mobility also challenges educational institutions to teach students to become more adaptive. The traditional American story was that we went to school to prepare ourselves for a career, whether as an auto mechanic or a doctor. We would settle on a career sometime during high school or college and take courses geared toward success in that career. In the 1980s and 1990s, however, the erosion of corporate responsibility for lifetime employment sparked increased job mobility across the economy. Currently, 50 to 60% of new hires leave their jobs within the first year, and 10% of the workforce leaves their jobs every year.[7] As we live longer, it turns out that many of us may be working into our 70s and 80s. Most Americans in the next 20 years will likely have a succession of careers.

As an example, one of the authors started his career as an auditor on Wall Street after getting a college degree in accounting. After a few years as an auditor, he returned to graduate school in computer science and 10 years later graduated with a Ph.D. in cognitive psychology. After that, he went to work in a firm that carried out research for the federal government in a variety of areas, most related to the use of computers in society. In his research work, he slowly moved from carrying out psychological research to developing computer systems for education. After some 20 years in research, he joined the education faculty at Northwestern, never having taken an education course during his career. Then, for 18 more years, he taught a variety of education courses at Northwestern. The second author started out as a graduate student in philosophy. He took a job as a history teacher in a small Chicago school. After several years of teaching, he became an administrator at the school. Later, he decided to return to graduate school in education. After 5 more years in graduate school, he became a professor at a large graduate school of education. It remains to be seen what he will do next. These stories, although they focus on academic careers, are not unusual. Such twists and turns in careers are becoming more and more common. The fate of people in a knowledge society, it seems, is that they must keep reinventing themselves in order to keep up with the changing world around them.

Eventually, people will come to think of life as made up of a succession of careers. In order to cope with this idea, they will begin to see how important it is to "learn how to learn." They may come to see that the career they decide to pursue in their early years is not a commitment for life. As Avner Avituv and Robert Lerman point out, "Every month, millions of workers leave one employer and take a job with another employer. It takes young workers a long time to enter a stable career and a long-term relationship with an employer. By the age of 30, high school graduates with no college have already worked for an average of eight employers. Nearly half of all male high school graduates experienced at least one spell of unemployment between ages 25–29. Moreover, job instability is increasing among young men."[8]

In recent years, there has been a growing gap between the incomes of college graduates and high school graduates. This has led over 90% of high school students to plan to go to college. But only 14% of kids with a C average in high school will complete a college degree.[9] They would be better off working for a few years after they finish high school and then going back to get more education. The success in college of returning veterans after World War II testifies to the payoff in waiting to go to college. A study by Norman Frederiksen found that the veterans had higher achievement levels than non-veterans.[10] Some of the pressure to go right on to college will be relieved if people come to understand that their life in the future will likely alternate between working and learning. It will no longer be 15 or 20 years of preparation followed by 30 years of working. Rather, we will learn for a while, work for a while, back and forth, until we retire.

Of course, some people in the future may be actors or auto mechanics for all of their lives. But they will be the exceptions. Thinking of a single career as the standard pattern leads people to think that they are done with learning when they finish school. So they do not keep their minds open and focused on continuing their learning. This makes them less adaptable when they are hit with the necessity of changing careers. Parents also need to understand how the nature of people's careers has changed, and not try to force young people to prepare for a particular career that they think is best for them. As a society, we need to build policies that support people in making the many career transitions they will have to make in a constantly changing environment.

RETHINKING THE TRANSITIONS BETWEEN LEARNING AND WORK

America has not helped its citizens manage the transition to adulthood as well as other countries with apprenticeship systems. Both high school graduates who don't enter college and students who drop out of college early have entered the workforce unprepared. Since only about 30% of students in America ever get a college degree, the vast majority of students have a more difficult transition to make. Typically, they drift from job to job until they are 25 or 30. Some return to college when they are older, but it is often harder for these students because society does not support older people returning to college. Given the increasing centrality of technology in work and the fact that people are more and more likely to change careers several times during their lifetime, it is worth rethinking the ways that society supports the transitions between learning and work.

The transition to work is handled fairly well when people graduate from college. The colleges maintain an office designed to help students find jobs, both as interns during college and when they graduate. This office has extensive files on employers in their area and many have files on alumni employed in different occupations who can guide students in choosing a career. Different employers come to colleges to recruit graduating students who are interested in working for them. Often, college students intern for different employers during the summers or during one of their later semesters, building ties with potential employers after they graduate. And college professors often write letters of recommendation for their students, even pointing them to potential employers. High school career centers and teachers sometimes perform this function, but it is sporadic and concentrated in wealthier communities. So there is an effective system in place, but only for college graduates.

In an era of multiple careers, people will need support to navigate their options, both in going from learning to work and from work to learning. If America wants to remain a successful society, it needs to create new ways to support citizens through these challenging transitions.

We believe America must transform how we address technical and vocational education. For example, schools should reconsider how to support teenagers who want to go into the job market, either in addition to or instead of going to high school. Teenagers should not go to work until they have mastered the basic skills and knowledge taught in middle school. Hence, there needs to be an office in high schools that determines whether teenagers have met the standards for going to work and that helps them find jobs that are well suited to their goals and abilities. This office would keep files of possible jobs, just as college employment offices do. It would help students put together resumes and assess their interests and abilities. It would also help gather teacher recommendations and make initial contacts with employers. In short, the office would carry out many of the same functions as college employment offices, but would provide more guidance, since the students are younger. Modest federal funding in this area would provide significant value in helping students make a successful transition between learning and work.

The same office might administer apprenticeship programs, such as are widely found in Europe.[11] In these programs, adolescent students typically work 3 days a week and go to school for 2 days a week. The programs attempt to coordinate what students are learning in school with the work for which they are training. Given the aimlessness of much work that teenagers are now doing, society would be well advised to put federal money into supporting a robust apprenticeship system. The office might also support students who have gone to work and wish to return to full- or part-time learning. The office could advise them about their options, such as taking high school or community college classes, online courses, or courses administered by a local learning center.

Such offices can also serve adults, who need help in thinking about embarking on a new career or returning to get more education. These counseling offices might be maintained by the state in all high schools, or they might be privately run. They would have counselors who can advise people on the kind of training and credentials they need to pursue a particular career, and what kind of educational resources are available to pursue that training. Other counselors could assess the skills and interests of adults to guide them toward viable careers they might pursue. Still other counselors would have knowledge and contacts with employers in the region, and could help people find jobs that suit them, given their educational background. These are resources we need to be providing to people to make our society as productive as possible.

Our view is that the government should pay for these learning resources, at least up to the level of what would be spent on a high school education. School-to-work programs, such as the School-to-Work Opportunities Act of 1994, provide a good start toward institutionalizing these types of services. Unfortunately, in recent years, these modest initiatives have been gutted by budget cuts. In 2006 alone, the Bush administration proposed to cut $1.1 billion in state vocational education grants. Cutting these transitional services means that the students with the least social capital, who need the most help connecting to viable economic resources, are left to make their own connections. There are so many alternatives that it is bewildering for most people, so they need counseling to make wise decisions. We will all profit from others learning all they can and finding employment that suits them.

RETHINKING EDUCATIONAL LEADERSHIP

We are experiencing a time of educational transition, which demands a new kind of educational leadership—a new Horace Mann, as it were. We need a vision of education that makes it possible for the new array of educational resources to reach all of the people. The trends in place are reaching the elites, and leaving behind the vast majority of people. The next generation of education leaders will need to face the political and technological challenges. The challenges of changing a well-established, entrenched institution are far different than those faced by Horace Mann. Parents, teachers, policymakers, and local communities all have compelling reasons to preserve the current system. The forces for change, such as the civil rights emphasis on using schools to increase social equity and the technological emphasis to open the core practices of schooling to information technologies, push uncomfortably against influential conservative forces. Leaders who can effect real change need to understand where the leverage points are to move the system, and need to have the organizational skills to bring together the resources and skills necessary to create change.

One possibility is to promote the inexpensive computer as a tool that can put powerful computing in the hands of all students. Such machines provide access to a vast array of educational resources for nonelites. Programs such as One Laptop Per Child[12] are currently aimed only at Third World nations, though they could be expanded to address poor people wherever they live. But we need to think much more broadly to address the inequities that are arising. Simply inserting technology into classrooms and schools without considering how the contexts for learning need to change will likely fail. Schools are still hesitant to embrace new technologies as a backlash from the significant, and largely ineffectual, investment in classroom computers as an instructional panacea in the mid-1990s.[13] Leaders need to understand the limits of the new technologies in order to set appropriate expectations for their communities. They will need to think about how to bring coherence to the incoherent array of tools already in schools and in the world.

In the future, educational leadership will require more than just reforming schools. We need to think about how to integrate nonschool resources into learning environments, both supporting families in bringing these tools into their homes and in building wired learning centers in communities that reach those in need. We need to support robust language-rich resources, which very young kids can use to learn to read. We have such programs for computers now, where, for example, a kid can hear a Dr. Seuss story by pointing at the words or lines on the screen to have them read aloud. As the kids learn the sight-to-sound correspondences, they will pick up reading of their favorite stories on their own. These machines should include the best children's literature, covering a wide variety of genres and topics. They should also include arithmetic games that would teach basic mathematical operations to young kids. Every young kid should have such a machine, since busy parents often do not have the time to read with their children. It might begin to address the inequity that many kids face.

Elementary school should provide an array of technology-based supplementary services to help students who are having trouble. Such services are envisioned by the No Child Left Behind (NCLB) Act as extending current special education and student services programs. If a child is having difficulties in one of his school subjects—say writing, math, or geography—then the first course of action should be to provide the child with a customized diagnostic process that connects the student's learning needs with appropriate resources. Technologies can provide a wide variety of resources, such as computer-based learning programs or access to online tutoring. Technologies allow students to use programs at home with their families as well as at school. If the programs do not succeed completely, then the kids might be provided with specialized human tutoring, as NCLB envisions. But human tutoring is a costly option that may not be necessary in most cases.

After eighth grade, kids might follow different educational paths, depending on their own and their parents' choosing. For example, as an alternative to continuing on to a traditional high school, a student might take online courses at home or in a learning center, enter an apprenticeship program, take courses at a community college, or attend a Career Academy, like we see in cities such as Oakland, California. Kids might even work for a while and later return to get more education, when they are ready. Giving students such options will make them less likely to feel that high school is a prison they must endure until they are grown up enough to go out on their own.

When a person is 14 or older—however old he or she may be—he or she should have access to a personalized learning counselor, who can provide advice about available educational options. As learning becomes more critical for success in the world, people will need individual support from someone who knows their history and the particulars of their life. Again, technologies greatly expand the range of advice that counselors can use to guide learners. Counselors can direct learners to online resources that guide novices through the initial stages of career choice and development.

A first visit to a counselor should be free and routine for everyone when they reach age 14. Learning counselors would be trained and licensed by the state, just as medical doctors are. The goal would be to develop a learning plan to address each person's interests, needs, and abilities, which would be adapted over the years as the person changed jobs and acquired more knowledge and responsibilities. The learning plan might involve taking online courses, going to a learning center for specialized training, getting a technical certification in some area, joining an apprenticeship program, or learning from computer-based tutorials to enhance particular skills. In any case, the learner should check with his or her counselor at regular intervals to evaluate how things are going and to consider how the plan might be revised.

These examples show how educational leaders need to think about changing schools from within and about how learners can be linked to resources outside schools. Thinking more broadly about technologies can revive our ideas about equity and extend available resources to the nonelites in our society. Our proposals are merely suggestive of the issues that leaders should be considering. Because society has identified education with schooling, we are systematically overlooking many of the resources now available for helping minorities and other nonelites.

Further, society views education reform as something that applies to youth rather than to people of all ages. With a broader view of education, we can begin to think about how to provide educational resources even to people in their 40s, 50s, and 60s.

We are not going to fix education by fixing the schools. They have served us very well in the past, but they are a 19th-century invention trying to cope with a 21st-century society. This is the time for another Horace (or Leticia) Mann to step forward and lead the nation toward a new education system. Our new leaders will have to understand the affordances of the new technologies that have become available in recent years, and to watch for issues and technologies on the horizon. They will need to understand that learning does not start with kindergarten and end with a high school or college diploma—we need to design a coherent lifelong-learning system.

RETHINKING THE ROLE OF GOVERNMENT
IN EDUCATION

Historically, the states and towns have been responsible for education in America, with the federal government only playing a supplementary role. The federal government has carried out some programs, such as developing science and math curricula to make the nation more competitive or supporting poor children by providing resources in order to ensure greater equity among children. But teacher's salaries, curriculum materials, and administrative expenses were paid with local funds. When the federal government in recent years has imposed standards on the states and towns, many have regarded this as encroachment on the states' authority. States will try to protect their authority, and this is leading to a backlash against the No Child Left Behind Act.

As we have pointed out, the technological resources that have been developed in recent years introduce new inequities into the education system. Wealthier parents are buying tutoring, computers, and web access for their children, leaving poor children further behind than ever. The states simply do not have the resources to correct these imbalances. They get most of their monies for education from property taxes, and the fact that fewer and fewer households have children makes it very difficult to raise property taxes to pay for education. And the costs of schooling each child have increased rapidly in recent years.

Without stepping on the states' authority, the federal government can try to equalize educational opportunities for all citizens. It can provide robust machines that teach reading to young kids and inexpensive computers with access to the web for older kids. It can provide educational guidance and tutoring for those who cannot afford to buy these services. It can set up apprenticeship programs that help kids make the transition into adulthood, rather than wandering aimlessly, as many now do. It can pay for additional training when people want to change careers. These are all supplemental services that do not step on the states' authority in any way.

There is also an important new role for state government in bringing about a new vision of education for a technology-rich world. If our society is going to support new alternatives for pursuing education, the states need to rethink their mandates of keeping kids in comprehensive schools until they are 16 years old. If we are going to let teenagers pursue other options besides staying in high school, the states will need to specify what alternatives are acceptable instead of school and what requirements students must meet before pursuing each alternative.

For example, the state might mandate that a student must acquire a specific set of certificates, such as demonstrating an ability to read and do math at an eighth-grade level, before pursuing a full-time job or some other option as an alternative to high school. The states might also monitor the teen's performance in the job and require teens to attend a weekly class where they discuss what they have learned in their work. If the work is not serving as a learning experience for the teens, a guidance counselor may help them find a new job that is of more value to them. If students are taking online courses at a learning center or participating in an apprenticeship program, the state might monitor their progress in similar fashion. The state would still have a responsibility for teenagers, but at the same time, would give them more latitude in pursuing their own education.

We have outlined examples of possible responsibilities that governments could take on, but these are not definitive. Governments should provide guidance to students at the same time that they loosen the reins that are keeping kids in high school, which many of them feel is a kind of prison. It would be wise for governments to put more responsibility on learners to pursue their own learning, but at the same time, it is critical that governments not ignore their responsibility to provide equal access to educational resources for all citizens.

OUR VISION OF THE FUTURE

As education becomes more privatized and commercial, we risk losing the vision promulgated by Thomas Jefferson and Horace Mann of a society where everyone has an equal chance at a good education. Horace Mann was right in predicting that education could provide a path for everyone to become part of the elite. Universal schooling formed the basis for our middle-class society today. But the onset of technology, privatization, and increasing inequality of income is undermining this vision.

Making economic success the central outcome of schooling risks marginalizing the political and moral goals of education. Education is, in many ways, America's civic religion. We use education to work toward our national ideals of equality, opportunity, and democracy. As a society, we need to understand how to balance the need to use schools as engines of economic competition with our national commitment to equality of opportunity.

According to a recent survey from the Education Trust, America is the only industrialized country in which today's young people are less likely than their parents to earn a high school diploma.[14] Those of us who care about education should do whatever we can to see that our children are educated as best they can to live in a technology-rich society. Even those of us without children should pay attention to this trend. All of us depend on the next generation to support our social services, such as Social Security and Medicare. For the future of America and the welfare of our individual futures, it is important that our society invest in the next generation's education. It behooves all of us to work toward a more equitable system of education.

What role will technology play in our national story of equity and economic development? In the 19th century, Americans developed the public school system to institutionalize our national commitment to citizenship, while at the same time addressing the needs of urban families to care for and educate children in the midst of the Industrial Revolution. Our generation faces a similar, but radically new, design challenge. We are dealing with a mature, stable system of education designed to adapt to gradual change, but ill-suited to embrace radical change. The pace of technological change has outstripped the ability of school systems to adapt essential practices. Schools have fiddled with learning technologies on the margins of the system, in boutique innovations that leave core practices untouched. The emergence of new forms of teaching and learning outside of school threaten the identification of learning with formal schooling forged in the 19th century.

For education to embrace both equity and economic development, we believe that our leaders will have to stretch their traditional practices to embrace the capacity of new information technologies. This will require schools to forfeit some control over the learning processes, but will once again put the latest tools for improving learning in the hands of public institutions (as opposed to the hands of families and learners who can afford access).

Parents and citizens need to start pushing for this more expansive view of education reform. School leaders and teachers will need to understand how learning technologies work and how they change the basic interactions of teachers and learners. Technology leaders will need to work together with educators, not as missionaries bearing magical gifts, but as collaborators in creating new opportunities to learn. It will take a concerted effort to bring about such a radical change in thinking. If a broader view develops in society, leaders will emerge who can bring about the political changes necessary to make the new educational resources available to everyone. These new leaders will need to understand the affordances of the new technologies, and have a vision for education that will bring the new resources to everyone. We hope these leaders may be reading this book now, and that it can guide them in taking action to address the learning revolution that is upon us.

Notes

Preface

1. de Tocqueville, 2003.

Chapter 1

1. Zuboff, 1988.
2. Murnane & Levy, 1996, report that the gap for men increased from about $5,000 to $10,000 from 1979 to 1993, and the gap for women increased from about $4,000 to $10,000 over the same period. The Bureau of the Census reports that the gap for men increased from about $13,000 to $21,000 from 1990 to 2004, and the gap for women increased from about $10,000 to $16,000 over the same period. Available online at http://www.infoplease.com/ipa/A0883617.html.
3. As evidenced by the explosive growth of Sylvan Learning Centers and Kaplan Inc. See, for example, http://en.wikipedia.org/wiki/Sylvan_Learning and http://en.wikipedia.org/wiki/Kaplan,_Inc.

Chapter 2

1. Brown, 2007.
2. Ito, 2008; Knobel, 2008; Leander & Boldt, 2008.
3. Sadler, 1987. Most adults in America think the phases of the moon are caused by the shadow of the Earth. In fact, the phases are caused by the spatial relation between the sun and moon as seen from the Earth. As the moon goes around the Earth, when the moon is in the direction of the sun, we see a new moon, and when it is in the opposite direction from the sun, we see a full moon. Similarly, most adults in America think the seasons are caused by changes in the distance of the Earth from the sun. In fact, the seasons are caused by the angle of the sun's rays as they hit the earth. The Earth is tilted in its orbit as it goes around the sun, and so in our winter, the direct rays fall on the Southern Hemisphere, and in our summer, they fall on the Northern Hemisphere.

4. Packer, 1997.

5. Stallard & Cocker, 2001.

6. Daiute, 1985.

7. See, for example, Black, 2008; Ito et al., 2008.

8. Gee, 2003.

9. Anderson, Boyle, & Reiser, 1985; Koedinger & Anderson, 1998.

10. Lesgold et al., 1992.

11. Collins, 1991.

12. Brown, 1985.

13. Schank et al., 1994.

14. Horwitz & Christie, 2000; Hickey et al., 2003. The first versions of *Biologica* were called *GenScope*. The system is also described in an article that reports on an experimental evaluation of its effectiveness in teaching genetics.

15. Dede et al., 2004.

16. Gee, 2003; Squire, 2006; Squire & Klopfer, 2007.

17. Steinkuehler, 2008; Steinkuehler, 2006.

18. Csikszentmihalyi, 1990.

19. Olson, 1994; Eisenstein, 1979; Ong, 1982; Postman, 1982.

20. Eisenstein, 1979.

21. Jenkins, 2008.

22. Tyner, 1994.

23. Norman, 1988.

24. Collins, Neville, & Bielaczyc, 2000.

25. Schön, 1983.

26. Collins & Brown, 1988.

27. White & Frederiksen, 1998; White & Frederiksen, 2005.

28. Papert, 1980.

Chapter 3

1. D. Dwyer, 1995. Personal communication.

2. Quotes 1–6 are cited from Dave Thornburg's *Edutrends 2010*, 1992. Quote 7 is from classroom teacher, and quote 8 is from a judge at a student science fair.

3. Cuban, 1986.

4. Cuban, 2001.

5. Powell, Farrar, & Cohen, 1985.

6. Callahan, 1962; Metz, 1990; Tyack, 1974.

7. Cuban, 1984.

8. David, 1995. Personal communication.

9. Cohen, 1988a.

10. Cohen, 1988b.

11. Shulman, 1986.

12. "But Some Buts Are Being Voiced," an undated excerpt from a report of the Fund for the Advancement of Education, in file "Pittsburgh Television-WQED-WQEX 1950s" in the Pennsylvania Room, the Carnegie Library of Pittsburgh. Quoted in Levin & Hines, 2003.

13. Powell, Farrar, & Cohen, 1985.

14. Russell & Haney, 1997.

15. Norris & Soloway, 2003.

16. Carroll et al., 2005.

17. Black America Study, 2008. Accessed online at http://blackamericastudy .com/summary/.

18. Cohen, 1988a.

19. Postman, 1995.

20. Powell, Farrar, & Cohen, 1985.

21. Dwyer, Ringstaff, & Sandholtz, 1990.

22. Rosenbaum, 1989; Rosenbaum, 2001.

23. Cohen, 1988a.

24. Postman, 1982.

25. Roberts, Foehr, & Rideout, 2005.

26. Fullilove & Treisman, 1990.

Chapter 4

1. Cremin, 1977, p. 12.

2. Cremin, 1977, pp. 13–14.

3. Ong, 1982.

4. Latour, 1986.

5. Eisenstein, 1979.

6. Carlton, 1965, p. 9.

7. Carlton, 1965, p. 12.

8. Vinovskis, 1995, p. 7.

9. Vinovskis, 1995, p. 9.

10. Franklin's *Proposals Relating to the Education of Youth in Pensilvania*, 1749 (University of Pennsylvania). Available online at http://www.archives.upenn.edu/ primdocs/1749proposals.html.

11. Cremin, 1977, pp. 28–29.

12. Cremin, 1951, p. 29.

13. The Northwest Ordinance (1787). Available online at http://usinfo.state. gov/usa/infousa/facts/democrac/5.htm.

14. Cremin, 1951, p. 29.

15. Cremin, 1980, p. 108.

16. Cremin, 1977, pp. 42–43.

17. Tyack, 1974, p. 30.

18. Carlton, 1965.
19. Carlton, 1965, p. 45.
20. Vinovskis, 1995, p. 10.
21. Vinovskis, 1995, p. 10.
22. Olson, 1982.
23. Tyack, 1974, p. 33.
24. Tyack, 1974, pp. 44–45.
25. Tyack, 1974, p. 38.
26. Tyack, 1974, p. 19.
27. Farnham-Diggory, 1990.
28. Tyack & Cuban, 1995, p. 91.
29. Callahan, 1962, p. 129.
30. Tyack, 1974, pp. 44–45.
31. Cubberley, 1916, p. 338.
32. Quoted in Lagemann, 2000, p. 59 (from Joncich, 1968, p. 3).
33. Tyack & Cuban, 1995, p. 85.
34. Tyack & Cuban, 1995, p. 86.
35. Olson, 1982.
36. Powell, Farrar, & Cohen, 1985.
37. The National Center for Education Statistics (NCES) carried out its survey of crime indicators in 2007. Available online at http://nces.ed.gov/programs/crimeindicators/crimeindicators2007/.
38. The National Center for Education Statistics (NCES) carried out its survey of home schooling in 2003. Available online at http://nces.ed.gov/pubs2006/homeschool/.
39. The National Center for Education Statistics (NCES) survey on home schooling documented the continuing increase in home schooling and the role that religion plays as a motivation for home schooling.
40. According to NCES, the percentage of students attending private schools increased from 1993 to 2003 by 1.7%, from 9.1% to 10.8%. Available online at http://nces.ed.gov/fastfacts/display.asp?id=6.

Chapter 5

1. NCES, 2006.
2. NCES, 2003.
3. Farris, 1997.
4. Farris, 1997.
5. Holt, 1981.
6. Stevens, 2001.
7. Guterson, 1992
8. Saulny, 2006.

9. Hirsch, 1987.

10. Wiggenhorn, 1990.

11. Wiggenhorn, 1990.

12. Accenture was formerly called Andersen Consulting, which should not be confused with the accounting firm Arthur Andersen. Arthur Andersen, which collapsed during the Enron scandal, had separated from Andersen Consulting some years before the Enron collapse. Accenture has since prospered.

13. Campbell & Monson, 1994.

14. Nowakowski, 1994.

15. Brown & Duguid, 2000.

16. Maeroff, 2003.

17. Maeroff, 2003.

18. Maeroff, 2003.

19. A description of the Open University can be found online at http://en.wikipedia.org/wiki/Open_University.

20. Lewis, 2001.

21. Postman, 1982, 1985.

22. Papert, 1993.

23. Gee, 2003.

24. Squire, 2004.

25. Bruckman, 2002.

26. Castronova, 2002.

27. Brown & Thomas, 2006.

28. See http://cisco.netacad.net/public/academy/.

29. Levander, 2001.

Chapter 6

1. Rodriguez, 1982.

2. SCANS Commission, 1991.

3. Cuban, 1984.

4. Frederiksen, 1984.

5. Coleman, 1961.

6. Eckert, 1989.

7. Delpit, 1988, p. 289.

8. Ferguson, 2002.

Chapter 7

1. Brooks, 2004.

2. Carnoy & Levin, 1985, p. 2.

3. Murnane & Levy, 1996.

    4. Kraut et al., 1998.

    5. Putnam, 2000.

    6. Davies & Aurini, 2006.

    7. Lave, 1988.

Chapter 8

    1. See, for example, Hanushek & Raymond, 2005.

    2. See, for example, Jones, Jones, & Hargrove, 2003, or Amrein & Berliner, 2002.

    3. Orfield et al., 2004.

    4. Wald & Losen, 2005.

    5. Florida, 2004.

    6. Roberts, Foehr, & Rideout, 2005.

    7. SCANS Commission, 1991.

    8. Mislevy et al., 2002.

    9. Joseph, 2004.

    10. Shaffer, 2004, 2006.

    11. Brown & Thomas, 2006.

    12. Kozol, 2005.

    13. See, for example, American Youth Policy Forum, 2002.

    14. Neill et al., 2004.

    15. Cole, 2006.

Chapter 9

    1. Gibson, 1999.

    2. Hagel & Brown, 2005, p. 11.

    3. Tapscott, 1998, pp. 1–2.

    4. Gee, 2003, Ch. 4.

    5. Beck & Wade, 2004.

    6. Johnson, 2005.

Chapter 10

    1. Friedman, 2006.

    2. Orfield & Lee, 2007.

    3. Barron, 2006.

    4. Yazzie-Mintz, 2006; Hart, 2006.

    5. Squire, 2004.

    6. Darling-Hammond, Ancess, & Falk, 1995.

    7. Henkoff, 1996; Feller & Walz, 1996.

8. Avituv & Lerman, 2004.
9. Rosenbaum, 2001.
10. Frederiksen, 1950.
11. Hamilton, 1990; Olson, 1997.
12. See http://laptop.org/en/vision/index.shtml.
13. See, for example, Cuban, 2001.
14. Germeraad, 2008.

References

American Youth Policy Forum. (2002). *Florida Virtual School: The future of learning?* Available at http://www.aypf.org/forumbriefs/2002/fb101802.htm

Amrein, A. L., & Berliner, D. C. (2002). High-stakes testing, uncertainty, and student learning. *Education Policy Analysis Archives, 10*(18). Available at http://epaa.asu.edu/epaa/v10n18/

Anderson, J. R., Boyle, C. F., & Reiser, B. J. (1985). Intelligent tutoring systems. *Science, 228*, 456–468.

Avituv, A., & Lerman, R. I. (2004). *Job turnover, wage rates, and marriage stability: How are they related.* New York: Urban Institute. Available at http://www.urban.org/publications/411148.html

Barron, B. (2006). Interest and self-sustained learning as catalysts of development: A learning ecologies perspective. *Human Development, 49*(4), 193–224.

Beck, J. C., & Wade, M. (2004). *Got game: How the gamer generation is shaping business forever.* Cambridge, MA: Harvard Business School Press.

Black, R. W. (2008). *Adolescents and online fan fiction.* New York: Peter Lang.

Brooks, D. (2004) *On Paradise Drive: How we live now (and always have) in the future tense.* New York: Simon & Schuster.

Brown, J. S. (1985, Spring). Idea amplifiers: New kinds of electronic learning environments. *Educational Horizons*, 108–112.

Brown, J. S. (2007). Innovation and Technology: Interview. *Wired Magazine.* Available at http://www.johnseelybrown.com/wired_int.html

Brown, J. S., & Duguid, P. (2000). *The social life of information.* Cambridge, MA: Harvard Business School Press.

Brown, J. S., & Thomas, D. (2006, April). You play *Warcraft*? You're hired! *Wired Magazine, 14*(04). Available at http://wiredmag.com

Bruckman, A. (2002). Co-evolution of technological design and pedagogy in an online learning community. In S. Barab and J. Gray, Eds., *Designing virtual communities in the service of learning.* New York: Cambridge University Press.

Callahan, R. E. (1962). *Education and the cult of efficiency.* Chicago: University of Chicago Press.

Campbell, R., & Monson, D. (1994). Building a goal-based scenario learning environment. *Educational Technology, 34*(9), 9–14.

Carlton, F. T. (1965). *Economic influences upon educational progress in the United States, 1820–1850*. Richmond, VA: William Byrd Press (originally published in 1908 by the University of Wisconsin).

Carnoy, M., & Levin, H. (1985). *Schooling and work in the democratic state*. Stanford, CA: Stanford University Press.

Carroll, A. E., Rivara, F. P., Ebel, B., Zimmerman, F. J., & Christakis, D. A. (2005). Household computer and Internet access: The digital divide in a pediatric clinic population. *AMIA Annual Symposium Proceedings*, 111–115. Available at http://www.pubmedcentral.nih.gov/articlerender.fcgi?artid=1560660

Castronova, E. (2002). *Virtual worlds: A first-hand account of market and society on the Cyberian frontier*. CES Info Working Paper 618. Available at http://papers.ssrn.com/sol3/papers.cfm?abstract_id=294828

Cohen, D. K. (1988a). Educational technology and school organization. In R. S. Nickerson & P. Zodhiates (Eds.), *Technology and education: Looking toward 2020*. Mahwah, NJ: Lawrence Erlbaum Associates.

Cohen, D. K. (1988b). Teaching Practice: Plus ça change. . . . In P. Jackson (Ed.), *Contributing to educational change: Perspectives on research and practice* (pp. 27–84). Berkeley, CA: McCutchan.

Cole, W. (2006, August 13). Outsourcing your homework. *Time*. Available at http://www.time.com/time/magazine/article/0,9171,1226166,00.html

Coleman, J. S. (1961). *The adolescent society*. New York: Free Press.

Collins, A. (1991). Cognitive apprenticeship and instructional technology. In L. Idol & B. F. Jones (Eds.), *Educational values and cognitive instruction: Implications for reform* (pp. 119–136). Hillsdale, NJ: Lawrence Erlbaum Associates.

Collins, A., & Brown, J. S. (1988). The computer as a tool for learning through reflection. In H. Mandl and Lesgold (Eds.), *Learning issues for intelligent tutoring systems* (pp. 1–18). New York: Springer-Verlag.

Collins, A., Neville, P., & Bielaczyc, K. (2000). The role of different media in designing learning environments. *International Journal of Artificial Intelligence in Education, 11*, 144–162.

Cremin, L. A. (1951). *The American common school: An historic conception*. New York: Bureau of Publications, Teachers College, Columbia University.

Cremin, L. A. (1977). *Traditions of American education*. New York: Basic Books.

Cremin, L. A. (1980). *American education: The national experience 1783–1876*. New York: Harper & Row.

Csikszentmihalyi, M. (1990). *Flow: The psychology of optimal experience*. New York: Harper & Row.

Cuban, L. (1984). *How teachers taught*. New York: Longman.

Cuban, L. (1986). *Teachers and machines*. New York: Teachers College Press.

Cuban, L. (2001). *Oversold and underused: Computers in the classroom*. Cambridge, MA: Harvard University Press.

Cubberley, E. (1916). *Public school administration*. Boston: Houghton Mifflin.

Daiute, C. (1985). *Writing and computers.* Reading, MA: Addison-Wesley.

Darling-Hammond, L., Ancess, J., & Falk, B. (1995). *Authentic assessment in action: Studies of schools and students at work.* New York: Teachers College Press.

Davies, S., & Aurini, J. (2006). The franchising of private tutoring: A view from Canada. *Phi Delta Kappan, 88*(2), 123–128.

Dede, C., Nelson, B., Ketelhut, D., Clarke, J., & Bowman, C. (2004). Design-based research strategies for studying situated learning in a multi-user virtual environment. *Proceedings of the 2004 International Conference on Learning Sciences*, pp. 158–165. Mahwah, NJ: Lawrence Erlbaum Associates.

Delpit, L. (1988). The silenced dialogue: Power and pedagogy in educating other people's children. *Harvard Education Review, 58*(5), 280–298.

de Tocqueville, A. (2003). *Democracy in America and two essays on America* (G. E. Bevan, trans.). London: Penguin.

Dwyer, D. C., Ringstaff, C., & Sandholtz, J. (1990). *The evolution of teachers' instructional beliefs and practices in high-access-to-technology classrooms.* Paper presented at the annual meeting of the American Educational Research Association, Boston.

Eckert, P. (1989). *Jocks and burnouts: Social categories and identity in high school.* New York: Teachers College Press.

Eisenstein, E. L. (1979). *The printing press as an agent of change.* Cambridge, UK: Cambridge University Press.

Farnham-Diggory, S. (1990). *Schooling: The developing child.* Cambridge, MA: Harvard University Press.

Farris, M. (1997). *The future of home schooling.* Washington, DC: Regnery.

Feller, R., and Walz, G., (Eds.). (1996). *Career transitions in turbulent times: Exploring work, learning, and careers.* Greensboro, NC: ERIC Clearinghouse on Counseling and Student Services, (ED 398 519).

Ferguson, R. F. (2002). *What doesn't meet the eye: Understanding and addressing racial disparities in high-achieving suburban schools.* Special Edition Policy Issues Report. Oak Brook, IL: North Central Regional Educational Laboratory.

Florida, R. (2004). *The rise of the creative class: And how it's transforming work, leisure, community and everyday life.* New York: Basic Books.

Frederiksen, N. (1950). *Adjustment to college: A study of 10,000 veteran and nonveteran students in sixteen American colleges.* Princeton, NJ: Educational Testing Service.

Frederiksen, N. (1984). The real test bias. *American Psychologist, 39*(3), 193–202.

Friedman, T. L. (2006). *The world is flat: A brief history of the twenty-first century.* New York: Farrar, Straus, and Giroux.

Fullilove, R. E., & Treisman, P. U. (1990). Mathematics achievement among African American undergraduates at the University of California, Berkeley: An evaluation of the mathematics workshop program. *The Journal of Negro Education, 59*(3), 463–478.

Gee, J. P. (2003). *What video games have to teach us about learning and literacy.* New York: Palgrave Macmillan.

Germeraad, S. (2008). *"Counting on graduation": Most states are setting low expectations for the improvement of high school graduation rates.* Washington, DC: Education Trust. Available at http://www2.edtrust.org/EdTrust/Press+Room/countingongrad.htm

Gibson, W. (1999). National Public Radio Interview. Talk of the Nation. November 30, 1999. Available at http://www.npr.org/templates/story.php& storyId =1067220

Guterson, D. (1992). *Family matters: Why home schooling makes sense.* San Diego, CA: Harcourt Brace.

Hagel, J., & Brown, J. S. (2005). *The only sustainable edge: Why business strategy depends on productive friction and dynamic specialization.* Cambridge, MA: Harvard Business School Press.

Hamilton, S. F. (1990). *Apprenticeship for adulthood: Preparing youth for the future.* New York: Free Press.

Hanushek, E. A., & Raymond, M. E. (2005). Does school accountability lead to improved student performance? *Journal of Policy Analysis and Management, 24*(2), 297–327.

Hart, P. D. (2006). *Report findings based on a survey among California ninth and tenth graders.* Washington, DC: Peter D. Hart Research Associates. Available at http://www.connectedcalifornia.org/downloads/irvine_poll.pdf

Henkoff, R. (1996, January 15). So you want to change your job. *Fortune, 133*(1), 52–56.

Hickey, D. T., Kindfeld, A. C., Horwitz, P., & Christie, M. A. (2003). Integrating instruction assessment, and evaluation in a technology-supported genetics environment. *American Educational Research Journal, 40*(2), 495–538.

Hirsch, E. D., Jr. (1987). *Cultural literacy: What every American needs to know.* New York: Houghton-Mifflin.

Holt, J. (1981). *Teach your own.* New York: Delacorte Press.

Horwitz, P., & Christie, M. (2000). Computer based manipulatives for teaching scientific reasoning: An example. In M. J. Jacobson & R. B. Kozma (Eds.), *Learning the sciences of the twenty-first century: Theory reseach and design of advanced technology learning environments.* Mahwah, NJ: Lawrence Erlbaum Associates.

Ito, M. (2008). Introduction. In K. Varnelis (Ed.), *Networked publics.* Cambridge, MA: MIT Press. Available at http://www.itofisher.com/mito/publications/

Ito, M., Horst, H., Bittanti, M., Boyd, D., Herr-Stephenson, B., Lange, P. G., Pascoe, C. J., & Robinson, L. (2008). *Living and learning with new media: Summary of findings from the Digital Youth Project.* Chicago: MacArthur Foundation Digital Media and Learning Project.

Jenkins, H. (2008). *Convergence culture: Where old and new media collide.* New York: NYU Press.

Johnson, S. B. (2005). *Everything bad is good for you: How today's popular culture is actually making us smarter.* New York: Riverhead Press.

Joncich, G. (1968). *The sane positivist: A biography of Edward L. Thorndike.* Middletown, CT: Wesleyan University Press.

Jones, G., Jones, B., & Hargrove, Tracy. (2003). *The unintended consequences of high stakes testing.* Lanham, MD: Rowman & Littlefield.

Joseph, D. (2004). The practice of design-based research: Uncovering the interplay between design, research, and the real-world context. *Educational Psychologist, 39*(4), 235–242.

Koedinger, K. R., & Anderson, J. R. (1998). Illustrating principled design: The early evolution of a cognitive tutor for algebra symbolization. *Interactive Learning Environments, 5*(2), 161–180.

Kozol, J. (2005). *The shame of a nation: The restoration of apartheid schooling in America* (pp. 39ff). New York: Three Rivers Press.

Knobel, M. (2008). *Studying animé music video remix as a new literacy.* Paper presented at the Annual Meeting of the American Educational Research Association, New York.

Kraut, R. E., Patterson, M., Lundmark, V., Kiesler, S., Mukophadhyay, T., & Scherlis, W. (1998). Internet paradox: A social technology that reduces social involvement and psychological well-being. *American Psychologist, 53*(9), 1017–1032.

Lagemann, E. L. (2000). *An elusive science: The troubling history of educational research.* Chicago: University of Chicago Press.

Latour, B. (1986). Visualization and cognition: Thinking with eyes and hands. In *Knowledge and society: Studies in the sociology of culture past and present (Vol. 6)* (pp. 1–40). New York: JAI Press.

Lave, J. (1988). The culture of acquisition and the practice of understanding (Report No. IRL88-0007). Palo Alto, CA: Institute for Research on Learning.

Leander, K., & Boldt, G. (2008). *New literacies in old literacyskins.* Paper presented at the Annual Meeting of the American Educational Research Association, New York.

Lesgold, A., Lajoie, S., Bunzo, M., & Eggan, G. (1992). Sherlock: A coached practice environment for an electronics troubleshooting job. In J. Larkin, R. Chabay, & C. Scheftic (Eds.), *Computer assisted instruction and intelligent tutoring systems* (pp. 201–255). Hillsdale, NJ: Lawrence Erlbaum Associates.

Levander, M. (2001, June 4). Where does fantasy end? Why all of South Korea is obsessed with an online game where ordinary folks can be arms dealers, murderers . . . and elves. *Time, 157* (22). Available at http://www.time.com/time/interactive/entertainment/gangs_np.html

Levin, R. A., & Hines, L. M. (2003). Educational television, Fred Rogers, and the history of education. *History of Education Quarterly, 43*(2) 262–275.

Lewis, M. (2001). *Next: The future just happened.* New York: W. W. Norton.

Maeroff, G. I. (2003). *A classroom of one: How online learning is changing our schools and colleges*. New York: Palgrave Macmillan.

Metz, M. H. (1990). Real school: A universal drama and disparate experience. In D. Mitchell & P. Goertz (Eds.), *Education politics for the new century: The twentieth anniversary yearbook of the Politics of Education Association*. Philadelphia: Falmer Press.

Mislevy, R., Steinberg, L., Breyer, F., & Almond, R. L. (2002). Making sense of data from complex assessments. *Applied Measurement in Education, 15*(2) 363–389.

Murnane, R. J., & Levy, F. (1996). *Teaching the new basic skills*. New York: Free Press.

National Center for Education Statistics. (2003). *Overview of public elementary & secondary schools & districts: 2001–02*. Washington, DC: U.S. Government. Available at http://nces.ed.gov/pubs2003/overview03/tables/table_9.asp

National Center for Education Statistics. (2006). *Homeschooling in the United States: 2003*. Washington DC: U.S. Government. Available at http://nces.ed.gov/pubsearch/pubsinfo.asp?pubid=2006042

Neill, M., Guisbond, L., Schaeffer, B., Madison, J., & Legeros, L. (2004). *Failing our children: How "No Child Left Behind" undermines quality and equity in education and an accountability model that supports school improvement*. Cambrige, MA: FairTest. Available at http://www.fairtest.org/files/chapter%20three%20-%20final%20color.pdf

Norman, D. A. (1988). *The design of everyday things*. New York: Currency/Doubleday.

Norris, C., & Soloway, E. (2003). The viable alternative: Handhelds. *School Administrator, 60*(4), 26–28.

Nowakowski, A. (1994). Reengineering education at Andersen Consulting. *Educational Technology, 34*(9), 3–8.

Olson, D. R. (1994). *The world on paper: The conceptual and cognitive implications of writing and reading*. Cambridge, UK: Cambridge University Press.

Olson, L. (1997). *The school to work revolution: How employers and educators are joining forces to prepare tomorrow's skilled workforce*. New York: Perseus.

Olson, M. (1982). *The rise and decline of nations*. New Haven, CT: Yale University Press.

Ong, W. J. (1982). *Orality and literacy: The technologizing of the word*. London: Routledge.

Orfield, G., & Lee, C. (2007, August 29). *Historic reversals, accelerating resegregation, and the need for new integration strategies*. Los Angeles: UCLA Civil Rights Project/Proyecto Derechos Civiles.

Orfield, G., Losen, D. J., Wald, J., & Swanson, C. (2004, February). *Losing our future: How minority youth are being left behind by the graduation rate crisis*. Cambridge, MA: The Civil Rights Project at Harvard University. Available at http://www.civilrightsproject.harvard.edu/research/dropouts/dropouts_gen.php

Packer, A. (1997). Mathematical competencies that employers expect. In L. A. Steen (Ed.), *Why numbers count: Quantitative literacy for tomorrow's America* (pp. 137–154). New York: College Entrance Examination Board.

Papert, S. (1980). *Mindstorms: Children, computers, and powerful ideas.* New York: Basic Books.

Papert, S. (1993). *The children's machine: Rethinking school in the age of the computer.* New York: Basic Books.

Postman, N. (1982). *The disappearance of childhood.* New York: Delacorte.

Postman, N. (1985). *Amusing ourselves to death: Public discourse in the age of show business.* New York: Viking Penguin.

Postman, N. (1995, October 9). Virtual students, digital classroom. *Nation,* 377–382.

Powell, A. G., Farrar, E., & Cohen, D. K. (1985). *The shopping mall high school: Winners and losers in the educational marketplace.* Boston: Houghton Mifflin.

Putnam, R. D. (2000). *Bowling alone: The collapse and revival of American community.* New York: Simon & Schuster.

Roberts, D. F., Foehr, U. G., & Rideout, V. (2005). *Generation M: Media in the lives of 8–18 year-olds.* Menlo Park, CA: The Henry J. Kaiser Family Foundation. Available at http://www.kff.org/entmedia/entmedia030905nr.cfm

Rodriguez, R. (1982). *Hunger of memory: The education of Richard Rodriguez.* New York: Bantam Books.

Rosenbaum, J. E. (1989, Winter). What if good jobs depended on good grades? *American Educator, 13*(3), 10–15, 40–42.

Rosenbaum, J. E. (2001). *Beyond college for all: Career paths for the forgotten half.* New York: Russell Sage.

Russell, M., & Haney, W. (1997). Testing writing on computers: An experiment comparing student performance on tests conducted via computer and via paper-and-pencil. *Education Policy Analysis Archives, 5*(3). Available at http://epaa.asu.edu/epaa/v5n3.html

Sadler, P. M. (1987). Misconceptions in astronomy. In J. Novak (Ed.), *Misconceptions and educational strategies in science and mathematics* (pp. 422–437). Ithaca, NY: Cornell University Press.

Saulny, S. (June 5, 2006). The gilded age of home schooling. *New York Times.*

SCANS Commision. (1991). *What work requires of schools: A SCANS Report for America 2000.* Washington, DC: The Secretary's Commission on Achieving Necessary Skills, U.S. Department of Labor.

Schank, R. C., Fano, A., Bell, B., & Jona, M. (1994). The design of goal-based scenarios. *Journal of the Learning Sciences, 3*(4), 305–346.

Schön, D. A. (1983). *The reflective practitioner: How professionals think in action.* New York: Basic Books.

Shaffer, D. W. (2004). Pedagogical praxis: The professions as models for post-industrial education. *Teachers College Record, 106*(7), 1401–1421.

Shaffer, D. W. (2006). *How computer games help children learn.* New York: Palgrave.

Shulman, L. (1986). Those who understand: Knowledge growth in teaching. *Educational Researcher*, February 1986. pp. 4–14.

Squire, K. D. (2004). Sid Meier's *Civilization III. Simulations and Gaming, 35*(1), 135–140.

Squire, K. (2006). From content to context: Videogames as designed experience. *Educational Researcher, 35*(1), 19–29.

Squire, K., & Klopfer, E. (2007). Augmented reality simulations on handheld computers. *Journal of the Learning Sciences, 16*(3), 371–413.

Stallard, C. H., & Cocker, J. S. (2001). *The promise of technology in schools: The next 20 years.* Lanham, MD: Scarecrow Press.

Steinkuehler, C. (2006). Virtual worlds, learning, & the new pop cosmopolitanism. *Teachers College Record, 12*(84).

Steinkuehler, C. (2008). Massively multiplayer online games as an educational technology: An outline for research. *Educational Technology, 48*(1), 10–21.

Stevens, M. L. (2001). *Kingdom of children: Culture and controversy in the home schooling movement.* Princeton, NJ: Princeton, University Press.

Tapscott, D. (1998). *Growing up digital: The rise of the net generation.* New York: McGraw-Hill.

Thornburg, D. D. (1992). *Edutrends 2010: Restructuring, technology, and the future of education.* San Carlos, CA: Starsong Publications.

Tyack, D. B. (1974). *The one best system: A history of American urban education.* Cambridge, MA: Harvard University Press.

Tyack, D., & Cuban, L. (1995). *Tinkering toward utopia: A century of public school reform.* Cambridge, MA: Harvard University Press.

Tyner, K. (1994). *Access in a digital age.* San Francisco: Strategies for Media Literacy.

Vinovskis, M. A. (1995). *Education, society, and economic opportunity: A historical perspective on persistent issues.* New Haven: Yale University Press.

Wald, J., & Losen, D. (2005, February). *Confronting the graduation rate crisis in the south.* Cambridge, MA: The Civil Rights Project at Harvard University. Available at http://www.civilrightsproject.harvard.edu/research/dropouts/dropouts_gen.php

White, B. Y., & Frederiksen, J. R. (1998). Inquiry, modeling, and metacognition: Making science accessible to all students. *Cognition and Instruction, 16*(1), 3–118.

White, B. Y., & Frederiksen, J. R. (2005). A theoretical framework and approach for fostering metacognitive development. *Educational Psychologist, 40*(4), 211–223.

Wiggenhorn, W. (1990). Motorola U: When training becomes an education. *Harvard Business Review,* July–August, 71–83.

Yazzie-Mintz, E. (2006). *Voices of students on engagement: A report on the 2006 high school survey of student engagement.* Available at http://ceep.indiana.edu/hssse/pdf/HSSSE_2006_Report.pdf

Zuboff, S. (1988). *In the age of the smart machine: The future of work and power.* New York: Basic Books.

Index

Brown, John Seely, 10, 86, 119, 122
Bruckman, Amy, 85–86

Callahan, Raymond, 32
Calvin, John, 51, 52
Cambridge Adult Education, 78
Canon, 74
Careers: and educational leadership,
  141–42; and learning centers, 80;
  rethinking, 135–37; and role of
  government, 143; and seeds of new
  system of education, 80; transitions
  in, 135–37. *See also* Work/work-
  place
Carlton, Frederick, 54, 55
Carnegie Foundation, 58
Carnegie units, 58, 61, 115
Carnegie-Mellon University, 107–8
Carnoy, Martin, 106
Castronova, Edward, 86
Center for Learning Technologies in
  Urban Schools (LeTUS), 118–19
Certification: and eras of education,
  94; national, 114–15, 116; and role
  of government, 144; and schools'
  coping with new technologies, 117–
  18; and seeds of new system of
  education, 66, 89–90; of teachers, 59;
  technical, 2, 66, 87–88, 89–90, 94
Charter schools: and control of
  education, 106; and eras of educa-
  tion, 94; and need for new vision of
  education, 129; and schools' coping
  with new technologies, 120; and
  seeds of new system of education,
  67, 68, 70, 77, 127
Cheating, 45
Children's Television Workshop
  (CTW), 82
Cisco, 2, 87
Cisco Networking Academy, 87
Civilization (game), 84–85, 119, 132

Claritas, 16
Classrooms: barriers to use of
  technology in, 39–40; impact of
  technology in, 127; management of,
  39–40, 48; and "one best system" of
  schooling, 32; and skeptics vision of
  schooling, 48
Co-opting of innovation, 36
Cocker, Julie, 17
Cohen, David, 34, 35–36, 39, 40–41, 43
Coleman, James, 101
College Board, 41, 121
Colorado Online Learning, 75
Committee of Ten, 58, 95
Communication: and changes in how
  we communicate, 11–13; development of new models of, 26; and
  integration of technologies into
  practices, 123; and multimedia, 24–
  25; and rethinking learning, 133–34;
  and schools' coping with new
  technologies, 119
Communities: and changes in ways of
  communicating, 11–13; and decline
  in sense of community, 108; and
  enthusiasts' vision of schooling, 28;
  interest-based, 11–13, 26; of place,
  11–13
Community learning centers, 80–81,
  101
Compulsory education, 60, 92
Computer adaptive testing, 115–16
Computers/Web: access to, 88–89,
  100, 106, 132; advantages and
  disadvantages of, 24, 40, 103; and
  enhanced capabilities for educating
  learners, 13–14; and flexibility of
  technologies, 34–35; and how
  education is changing, 5–6; impact
  on schools of, 32, 43–47; lack of, 9–
  10; and losses from educational
  revolution, 106; as means for

About the Authors

Allan Collins is professor emeritus of education and social policy at Northwestern University. He is a member of the National Academy of Education and a fellow of the American Association for Artificial Intelligence, the Cognitive Science Society, the American Educational Research Association, and the American Association for the Advancement of Science. He served as a founding editor of the journal *Cognitive Science* and as first chair of the Cognitive Science Society. He has studied teaching and learning for over 30 years, and has written extensively on related topics. He is best known in psychology for his work on how people answer questions, in the field of artificial intelligence for his work on reasoning and intelligent tutoring systems, and in education for his work on situated learning, inquiry teaching, design research, and cognitive apprenticeship. From 1991 to 1994, he was co-director of the U.S. Department of Education's Center for Technology in Education. Recently, he was chosen by French psychologists as one of 37 living scholars who have had the most impact on the field of psychology.

Richard Halverson (Ph.D., Northwestern University) is an associate professor of educational leadership and policy analysis at the University of Wisconsin-Madison. Halverson is nationally recognized for his research on documenting instructional leadership expertise in areas such as data-driven decision-making, urban school leadership, and teacher evaluation. Halverson is a former high school teacher, school technology specialist, curriculum director, and school administrator. He is a co-founder of Games, Learning and Society at the University of Wisconsin-Madison, an internationally known research group that investigates how cutting-edge learning technologies can reshape learning in and out of schools.